GETTING INTO........

BLUEGRASS MANDOLIN

by DIX BRUCE

Online Audio   www.melbay.com/20099BCDEB

Re-order from:
www.musixnow.com

Audio Contents

1. Intro [0:28]
2. How to Tune [1:10]
3. Tuning Tones [1:50]
4. Strum Demo [1:21]
5. Roll in My Sweet Baby's Arms S [0:41]
6. Roll in My Sweet Baby's Arms F [0:26]
7. Camptown Races example [0:15]
8. John Hardy S [0:51]
9. John Hardy F [0:33]
10. Will the Circle #1 S [0:45]
11. Will the Circle #1 F [0:33]
12. Bluegrass Rhythm [1:01]
13. Bluegrass Chop [1:48]
14. More Bluegrass Chop [1:22]
15. East Virginia Blues S [0:39]
16. East Virginia Blues F [0:25]
17. Bury Me Beneath the Willow S [1:09]
18. Bury Me Beneath the Willow F [0:51]
19. Long Journey Home S [0:37]
20. Long Journey Home F [0:23]
21. 3/4 Rhythm [0:49]
22. All the Good Times S [0:37]
23. All the Good Times F [0:27]
24. Aura Lee S [1:05]
25. Aura Lee F [0:47]

26. Pick Direction [1:26]
27. Old Joe Clark S [1:10]
28. Old Joe Clark F [0:40]
29. Ragtime Annie S [1:21]
30. Ragtime Annie F [0:45]
31. Liberty S [1:25]
32. Liberty F [0:52]
33. Nine Pound Hammer Basic [0:39]
34. Nine Pound Hammer Solo S [0:46]
35. Nine Pound Hammer Solo F [0:26]
36. Crawdad Song melody S [0:37]
37. Crawdad Song Solo S [0:38]
38. Crawdad Song Solo F [0:24]
39. Slides example [0:14]
40. Slides exercise [0:34]
41. Hammer example [0:32]
42. Hammer/Pull exercise [0:47]
43. When the Saints S [0:39]
44. When the Saints F [0:26]
45. Double Stop example [0:29]
46. Somebody Touched Me Basic S [0:35]
47. Somebody Touched Me Solo S [0:37]
48. Somebody Touched Me Solo F [0:26]
49. Will the Circle Solo S [0:41]
50. Will the Circle Solo F [0:30]

51. Will the Circle Substitution [0:51]
52. Bury Me Beneath Solo S [0:40]
53. Bury Me Beneath Solo F [0:28]
54. Solo Endings [0:37]
55. Tremolo Demo [0:39]
56. Banks of the Ohio Solo S [0:47]
57. Banks of the Ohio Solo F [0:33]
58. Down in the Willow Garden S [1:09]
59. Down in the Willow Garden F [0:45]
60. Pass Me Not S [1:40]
61. Pass Me Not F [1:03]
62. A Beautiful Life S [1:09]
63. A Beautiful Life F [0:48]
64. New River Train S [0:36]
65. New River Train F [0:25]
66. In the Pines S [0:45]
67. In the Pines F [0:31]
68. Lonesome Valley Basic S [0:37]
69. Lonesome Valley Basic F [0:29]
70. Lonesome Valley in D S [0:38]
71. Lonesome Valley in D F [0:27]
72. Lonesome Valley in C S [0:39]
73. Lonesome Valley in C F [0:28]
74. Little Maggie Basic [0:28]
75. Little Maggie Solo/G S [0:44]

76. Little Maggie Solo/G F [0:31]
77. Little Maggie Solo/A S [0:44]
78. Little Maggie Solo/A F [0:30]
79. Little Maggie Solo/C S [0:45]
80. Little Maggie Solo/C F [0:30]
81. Shady Grove Basic [0:29]
82. Shady Grove Solo S [0:27]
83. Shady Grove Solo F [0:19]
84. Wayfaring Stranger Basic [1:15]
85. Wayfaring Stranger Solo S [1:50]
86. Wayfaring Stranger Solo F [1:16]
87. Triplet demo Mix [0:38]
88. Moveable Blues in G S [0:43]
89. Moveable Blues in G F [0:32]
90. Moveable Blues in B♭ S [0:47]
91. Moveable Blues in B♭ F [0:32]
92. Man of Constant Sorrow Basic [0:34]
93. Man of Constant Sorrow Solo S [0:54]
94. Man of Constant Sorrow Solo F [0:36]
95. Man of Constant Sorrow Kick S [0:27]
96. Will the Circle Kicks S [1:04]
97. Bury Me Beneath Kicks S [0:55]
98. Last Kicks S [1:41]

"S" = slow version; "F" = version up to speed.

Special thanks to Tom Diamant, Tom Bekeny, and Gene Tortora for their excellent suggestions; to Lorna Joy Swain, Laura Alber and Bob Bergman for their help in proofing the manuscript. Photos by Gene Tortora.

3 4 5 6 7 8 9 0

Visit us on the Web at www.melbay.com — E-mail us at email@melbay.com

Table of Contents

Table of Contents

Foreword

Hello and welcome! The *Getting into Bluegrass Mandolin* book and audio set is specifically designed to get you up and playing bluegrass mandolin. We'll start out with some general mandolin topics and then dive directly into all the things you'll need to know to play bluegrass mandolin: chords, rhythm, single note playing, double stops, fiddle tunes, playing in all keys, playing backup, transposing from one key to another, introductions or kickoffs, and tremolo. We'll use classic bluegrass songs and tunes in the process so that by the end of this book, you'll have the beginnings of a great repertoire!

Before we get started let's define a few terms. What is "bluegrass music?" To me, the main ingredient in bluegrass is the music of mandolinist Bill Monroe, who is known as "the father of bluegrass." Bluegrass coalesced in the mid-1940s with Monroe's mixing of American old time, mountain, country, and blues. While Monroe wasn't the style's only creator, he certainly synthesized the sound we now know as bluegrass with his band The Bluegrass Boys. Since that time, hundreds of other individuals and groups have built on Monroe's innovations and made music in his general style. I would certainly consider the music of artists like Monroe, Ralph and Carter Stanley, Flatt & Scruggs, Jimmy Martin, The Country Gentlemen, Tony Rice, J.D. Crowe, etc., to be bluegrass.

Monroe's classic band was a quintet made up of mandolin, guitar, banjo, fiddle, and bass, all acoustic instruments, no drums. Much of the repertoire was made up of traditional songs and tunes, but Monroe penned many of the songs now considered classics. Folklorist Alan Lomax called bluegrass "folk music in overdrive," which I find to be a beautifully descriptive and accurate term. Bluegrass is built on a basic string band sound but one that is supercharged by the fierce backbeat of guitar and mandolin, the rolling motivation of the five-string banjo, and the hot and fast instrumental work of all the lead players.

As you'll see as we progress though this book, the role of the mandolin in bluegrass music encompasses a unique way of playing rhythm and leads. We'll explore bluegrass mandolin in depth in the pages to come. So let's have at it!

Dix Bruce, November 2004

Photo by Gene Tortora

The Mandolin and its Parts

Your mandolin is probably similar to one of two basic models: A-style or F-style. If you're playing a round-back or "taterbug," its face will be similar to the A-model. Take a look at the diagram below and familiarize yourself with the different parts of the mandolin. Read through the text and find out why these parts are important. You should know the difference between a headstock and an end pin. You can always refer back to this diagram as we explore the mandolin in more depth.

1. **Bridge.** Strings rest on the bridge, which conducts their vibration to the resonant top of the mandolin. Nearly all mandolin bridges "float," held onto the top only by the tension of the strings. As such, bridges move and may need to be corrected periodically to insure proper tuning and intonation. Some bridges are height adjustable by two small wheels imbedded in the bridge itself.

2. **End Pin.** The end pin holds one end of your strap. If you have an F-style mandolin, use a leather lace or strap and tie the other end of the strap around the curl. If your mandolin doesn't have a curl, tie the other end onto the headstock (6), under the strings near the nut (8).

3. **F-hole.** F-holes are sound holes shaped like a script letter *"f"* as on a violin. After the music goes round and round, it comes out here. Other mandolins, like the A-style, have oval-shaped sound holes (see #12 below).

4. **Fretboard or Fingerboard.** This is where your fingers press the strings to make different notes and chords. Always place your fretting finger in the space between the metal frets, not on the metal frets themselves.

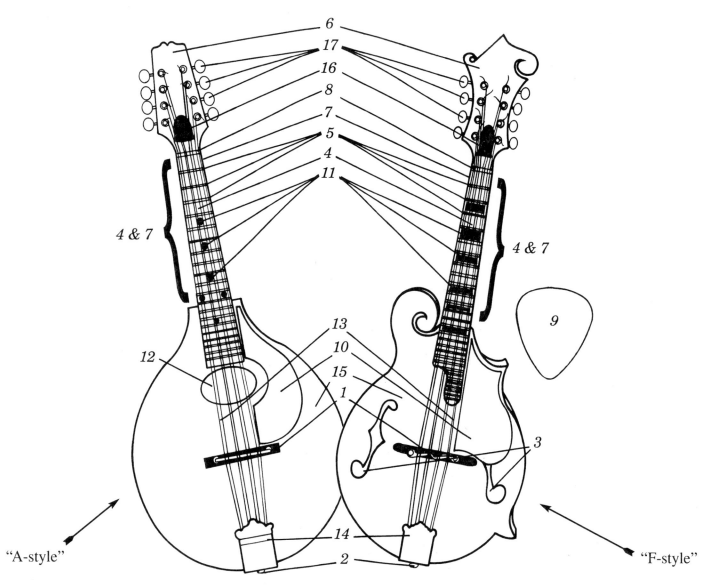

5. **Frets.** Frets are the actual metal wires that delineate the fret spaces. When we refer to "fret one" we mean the space between the nut and the first fret wire. When we refer to "fret two" we mean the space between the first and second fret wires. Remember, put your fingers in the space, not on the fret wire!

6. **Headstock.** The headstock holds the tuning gears (17) which anchor one end of the strings. The other end of the strings, which has a loop, is anchored to the tailpiece (14).

7. **Neck.** The neck connects the headstock with the body of the instrument and holds the fingerboard and strings. "The neck bone's connected to the headstock…"

8. **Nut.** The other point besides the bridge where the strings rest is the nut. The nut sits between the headstock and the end of the fingerboard, and is slotted so the strings don't wander. It's usually made of bone, ivory, or plastic.

9. **Pick.** The pick or plectrum is the little piece of plastic you use to contact the strings when you strum or play single notes to make noise/music. Picks come in a variety of shapes, sizes, and thicknesses. Get several to try out. Stay away from thin picks. They give a floppy, clicky, sound that isn't used in bluegrass. (Shown much larger than life.)

10. **Pickguard.** A pickguard protects the top of your mandolin from pick scratches and gouging. Bluegrassers often remove their pickguards. The result can be a rapidly dissolving mandolin.

11. **Position Markers.** These are the mother-of-pearl or painted dots and decorations on the front and side of the fingerboard which help you tell, at a glance, one fret from another. You'll usually find them on frets five, seven, nine, twelve and fifteen. Fret twelve usually has two. Most mandolins also have markers on the side of the neck so you can tell positions with a side-long glance.

12. **Soundhole.** The oval-shaped opening on A-style mandolins. See "F-holes" above.

13. **Strings.** The mandolin has eight strings tuned in pairs to the same pitches as violin strings: E-A-D-G, from highest to lowest pitch, from right to left as you look at the fingerboard. Strumming or picking the strings makes them vibrate. These vibrations are in turn amplified by the top of the instrument. We usually refer to each pair of strings as one string. The thinnest and highest pitched string is "string 1," the thickest and lowest pitched is "string 4." I like phosphor bronze strings and have used them exclusively for over thirty years. By the way, they're not really strings at all, they're wires.

14. **Tailpiece and Cover.** This is where the loop-ends of the strings not attached at the headstock are anchored. Strings often rattle and buzz here. To remedy this, weave a thin piece of leather or felt through the strings, between the bridge and tailpiece. If the tailpiece cover rattles, place a thin piece of leather or felt between the tailpiece and tailpiece cover.

15. **Top or Soundboard.** The top is the main vibrating element of the mandolin. It has to be strong enough to survive the tremendous pressure the strings exert on it, while supple enough to easily resonate and amplify the string vibrations. The quality of the top, a trade-off between strength and resonance, most determines the quality of the sound of the instrument.

16. **Trussrod Cover.** Many mandolins have necks reinforced with a metal trussrod. Most of these rods are adjustable (best done by a repair professional) under the trussrod cover, to correct the neck warp that time, weather, and string pressure often cause. The trussrod cover is a plate, usually plastic, which cosmetically covers this adjustment point.

17. **Tuning Gears.** Tuning gears tighten or loosen string tension to raise or lower the pitch of the strings to tune the mandolin.

Holding the Mandolin

In the next section, we'll talk a bit about the basics of holding and playing the mandolin. If you are an absolute beginner and would like more general information about the mandolin, check out my *First Lessons Mandolin* book/CD set (99945BCD) and *You Can Teach Yourself Mandolin,* book/CD/video/DVD (94331BCD), both published by Mel Bay and available on my website: www.musixnow.com.

Your mandolin should sound fairly good and be relatively easy to play, though it may be difficult for you to determine that at this point. If you're a complete beginner just about everything can seem difficult to play and may not sound good! It would be worth your while to consult a local instrument repair person to make sure that your mandolin is set up well enough to give you a fighting chance at playing it.

I recommend that students always play with a strap. A strap will help you maintain a constant playing position whether you are sitting or standing. (See photos.) Your mandolin should

have an end pin protruding from the bottom of the body, opposite from the headstock, around which one end of your strap will attach. As I mentioned in #2 above, if you have an F-style mandolin, the other end of the strap goes around the curl. If your mandolin doesn't have a curl, tie the other end onto the headstock (6), under the strings near the nut (8). Use a leather or fabric lace. My strap is a simple and thin piece of leather. You can make your own from stock bought at a leather or shoe shop. Commercial straps usually have adjusting buckles. It's best to avoid this type of strap as it'll bang against your mandolin and scratch it.

Cradle your mandolin gently in your fretting hand. Lightly place the thumb on the side of the back of the neck (the mandolin's, not yours!). Your fingers should reach around to the fingerboard. The strap should go all the way around both of your shoulders, not just off the one. Bluegrassers tend to use the "one shoulder" technique which developed because most of the early mandolin and banjo players wore western hats and they would have had to take their hat off to put the strap over their head. While the one shoulder technique is convenient hat-wise, it can lead to a lot of tension and stress as that shoulder holds the mandolin in position.

Whether you're sitting or standing, find a comfortable and relaxed position for your upper body and arms. Everybody feels a little tight at first, but your ultimate goal is to relax your shoulder, arm, and hand muscles so there's a minimum of stress in those areas. The less stress, the easier it will be to play and the longer you'll be able to play.

When you fret strings, make contact with the tips of your fingers. Over time you'll develop calluses on your fretting fingertips and this is a good thing. Your fingertips will get sore in the process but that means that calluses are in the making. On some of the chord photos it may look as though my fingers are get-

7

ting dangerously close to the fret wires. Since we're friends, I'll admit something to you: I have big fat fingers and big fat fingertips. However, I've developed healthy calluses on my fingertips and have learned how to place them in the frets so I get a nice clean ringing sound without too many thuds or buzzes. If I can do it with my chubby fingers, you can do it with yours! It just takes a little practice.

Holding the Pick

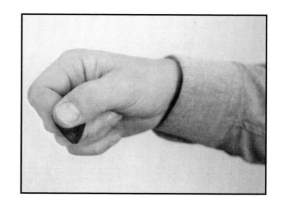

Hold the pick loosely in your picking hand. You only need to apply enough pressure to hold onto it as you strum. No doubt it will fly out of your hand from time to time but this will help you determine how much pressure is enough. Again, as with your shoulders and arms, you want to keep your picking hand as loose as possible. Stress will only cause fatigue and cramping and can slow you down.

It may help your accuracy to brush the pick guard or top of the mandolin with the fourth finger of your picking hand. A controversy rages as to whether to do this or not. Proponents say that brushing increases accuracy; opponents say it may ultimately slow a player down, especially if the pinkie gets planted on the top of the mandolin. See the photos.

Picking—Pinkie brush.

Picking—No pinkie.

Picks

I suggest that you try picks in a variety of shapes and thicknesses. Most players I know settle on some type of heavy pick. I use a standard Fender heavy. I'm used to them, and they are widely available. Stay away from real tortoise shell picks. They're expensive, illegal, and they come from an endangered species. *Dawg Picks* are currently in vogue. They are super stiff and David Grisman designed them to simulate the sound and feel of tortoise shell. *(For Dawg Pick info: www.musixnow.com).*

Tuning the Mandolin

Mandolins are tuned like violins, except that violins have only one string for each pitch, and mandolins have two. Each string in the pair is tuned to one of the notes shown below. Tune to the tones at the beginning of the CD, use an electronic tuner, or tune to the piano. Tuning notes on the piano are shown below. Start with string #1, the E (thinnest string) and get one of the pair in tune to your source, then tune the other in the pair to it. Listen to the "How to Tune" on the CD.

Getting your mandolin in tune requires lots of practice and listening. Be sure to work on it every time you play your instrument. It will develop over time. If you can't hear what's in tune yet, don't worry about it, but have someone help you tune your mandolin from time to time. The most popular and probably the most effective tuner for an acoustic mandolin is the *Intellitouch,* which clips on the mandolin headstock and senses the vibrations of the strings.

If you don't have access to any reliable tuning tones, you can still get your mandolin in tune with itself. First you have to decide which of the strings is most in tune and tune the others to it. Let's assume that the first string E (far right as you look at the fingerboard and thinnest) is the closest to being correct. Fret the second string (A) at the seventh fret and match that fretted sound of the second string to the sound of the open first string. When these match you'll have strings one and two in tune. Now fret the third string (D) at the seventh fret and match that fretted sound to the sound of the newly tuned open second string. Finally fret the fourth string (G) at the seventh fret and match that fretted sound to the sound of the newly tuned open third string. Use this "fretted/open-string" method whenever you need to check your tuning.

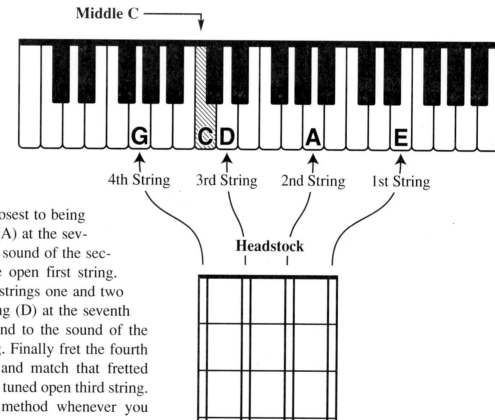

9

Chord Diagrams

We'll learn chords from chord diagrams like the one shown here. The vertical lines of the chord diagram represent the strings on your mandolin, right to left, strings one through four. The horizontal lines represent the fret wires. The numbers in the grid tell us which fingers to use to fret the individual strings. Fretting finger numbers are as follows: 1 = index; 2 = middle; 3 = ring; 4 = pinkie. (See photo below. I had these numbers tatooed on my fingertips when I was just a little picker, but I don't recommend it.) If you see a little "x" below or above one of the strings, don't play that string.

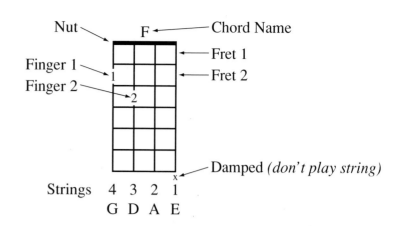

Chords

It's important that you memorize chords as you are introduced to them. Chords are like words, and you'll need to build a vocabulary of them in order to speak musically. Once you can play just a few chords and understand how to read chord diagrams you'll be able jump right in and play songs in just about any style. You'll be able to read chords from any source: guitar or piano books from your favorite bands — anything that includes chords — and play along. Even lyric sheets from the internet. By the way, I have downloadable mandolin music with chords and tablature posted on my website: www.musixnow.com.

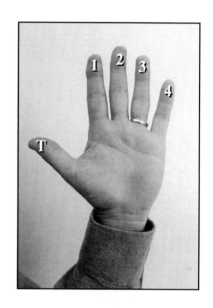

Unless you're reading from a book specifically designed for mandolin players, the music will probably not show you the actual mandolin chord diagrams like the ones shown above. If you memorize the chords, you won't find that to be a limitation. That's because a G chord on the piano is the same as a G on the guitar or the mandolin! Sure, you finger them differently, but as I said, they are all G chords or Cm chords, or B7 chords.

How to Use the CD

One of the easiest and best ways to practice the mandolin is to play along with me on the CD. Listen before you play. Most songs will be on the CD at two speeds; slow and regular. Some of the basic melodies we developed into solos are only presented at the slow speed. Same with the kickoffs at the end of the book. (If you want to hear the full speed versions, they can be downloaded from the download area of my website: www.musixnow.com.)

Musical examples include rhythm guitar, which is panned to stereo center. Lead parts will generally be panned to the right channel, rhythm to the left. By adjusting the balance control on your stereo, you can isolate the parts for study or playing along. If you're listening with headphones, take off the side you don't want to hear.

You may find it difficult to play along with the CD, especially in the beginning, so be patient and work your way up first to the slow version of each song, then to the regular speed version. Use the CD to first demonstrate how each song should sound, practice it on your own, then as you progress, play along with the CD to master chords and melodies. One of the nice features of a CD is that you can set it up to automatically repeat a track as many times as you wish. Doing this will help build your strength, endurance, and speed.

It may take you awhile to work your way up to playing with the slow or regular speed version but the best thing you can do is play, play, play! Every day is best. If you can only manage fifteen minutes the first few days, that's OK, just keep trying to play longer each day. Playing along with me on the CD will also get you used to playing with other people.

Try to play through all the verses to a song on your own. Since we have only a limited amount of time available on a CD, we can only include one or two verses. But, the more verses you sing and play, the faster you will progress, and the more verses you learn, the more repertoire you'll have to perform.

Let's Play!/First Chords, First Song

Before we get into specifically "bluegrass" mandolin, let's review some general mandolin chords. If you're relatively new to mandolin, you know or are just learning chords like these:

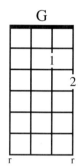
G

C

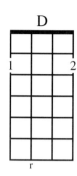
D

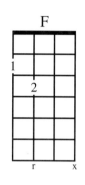
F

These types of chords are known as "open chords" because along with the fretted notes, they also have open-string notes. We strum all four strings on chords like these and let them all ring out. The one exception above is the F chord, where we either mute or avoid playing string number one, shown in the chord diagram with an "x" below the first string. When I play the F chord, I do a combination of both: I mute the first string with the soft part of my first fretting finger and try to not pick the string.

Though bluegrass mandolinists don't generally use these types of open-string chords, they are an option, and have a characteristic ringing sound. In classic bluegrass mandolin rhythm we usually play "closed string" chords with no open or unfretted strings. We'll get to "closed" chords next.

In the bluegrass context open-string chords have a couple of drawbacks. One is that with open strings, you can't stop the ringing of picked strings to emphasize the chordal rhythm or "chop." A second disadvantage is that open-string chords are not moveable up and down the fingerboard like closed chords. With closed chords we can learn one shape and move it up and down the fingerboard to eight or more different positions and chords.

In addition to the small letter "x" under the F chord grid, all the grids have a small "r" under one or more of the strings. The string with the "r" below it tells us where the "root" note of that particular lies in the chord. The root of a chord names it. For example, the root of the C chord is a C note. When we get to closed position chords, knowing the chord's root and the names of the notes on the fingerboard will take on greater importance. As you'll see, some chords will have two roots, some will have none.

Before we get into closed position bluegrass chop chords, let's play through a song with open chords to warm up and also accustom our ears to hearing the difference between "open" and "closed" chords. Be sure to listen to "Roll in My Sweet Baby's Arms" in the key of G on the CD and strum along. Plug in the G, C and D chords above where shown in the music below. If you're going to play bluegrass, you need to know this song. We'll learn a lead part on it later in the book.

We'll use a simple single down-stroke strum across all of the strings except those shown in the chord diagrams with an "x," on these first few songs. Listen to the demonstration on the CD. After you've practiced the chords and can play them from memory, play along with me on the CD. Most of the selections are recorded at both slow and regular speeds, and we'll play these first few at very moderate tempos. Work your way up from the slow speed versions to the regular speed. It's important that you get into the habit of playing along right away. Only by doing that can you hear how these songs should sound, and since the mandolin is such a social instrument, you'll want to develop the skill of playing with others. So play along with me. I promise I won't complain or even roll my eyes if you hit a wrong note or chord!

Keys

"Roll in my Sweet Baby's Arms" is written here in the key of G. Songs can be played or sung in a number of different keys: A, A♯/B♭, B, C, C♯/D♭, D, D♯/E♭, E, F, F♯/G♭, G, G♯/A♭. The slash between A♯ ("A sharp") and B♭ ("B flat") in A♯/B♭ means that A♯ and B♭ are actually the same keys. A♯ and B♭ are *enharmonic* names for the same key or note. We use different keys to accommodate different voice or instrument ranges. I have a pretty typical male voice, not very high, not very low. I might sing "Roll in My Sweet Baby's Arms" in the key of G while a person with a typical female voice might sing the same song in the key of C. As you'll see as we progress through this book, different keys offer different scale notes and accompaniment chords. For now, notice which chords are grouped together in which keys. In this case, "Roll in My Sweet Baby's Arms" in the key of G, you'll find the chords G, C, and D. In this book, a song's key will be listed in the upper left corner of the music.

Roll in My Sweet Baby's Arms

Tablature

Before we look into closed position chords, let's work on learning to play a couple of melodies. As with all the songs and examples in *Getting Into Bluegrass Mandolin* be sure to learn the chords **and** the melodies to each song, even if we only discuss one or the other.

Our first melody, "John Hardy," is written below in standard music notation on a five-line, four-space staff with quarter, half, and whole notes. Directly below is a line of tablature, a position-based notation system that uses a four-line staff representing the four strings on the mandolin, and numbers representing the frets on the individual strings.

Tablature is an alternative to music reading that shows the position of a note on the fingerboard. Tablature or "tab" shows fretted stringed instrument players where to fret notes. There are several different styles of tab and none is standard. Many styles of tab don't show how long to hold a given note, as does standard musical notation. Standard notation doesn't usually come with tab. Most of the "serious" music world reads and writes standard notation. If you learn to read it, you can play with millions of musicians of all kinds all over the world, from classical to jazz. It takes just about as long to learn to read notes as it does to read tablature.

On the other hand, tab can be very useful to players who are just beginning on their instruments and don't want to take the time to learn to read music. While tab can be helpful in showing a player exactly where a note is located on a fretboard or getting a beginner started, it can ultimately be very limiting if a player doesn't eventually move beyond a dependence on tab.

I suggest that you use tab to get started but if you only learn one system, standard notation will be much more useful in the long run. My "You Can Teach Yourself Mandolin" as a good place to start for learning basic music reading. Below is a brief explanation of the style of tab I use.

Numbers, which correspond to the fret where the note is played, are arranged on a four line staff, each line representing one of the strings on the mandolin. The top line of the tablature staff represents the first or highest pitched string (E) of the mandolin, second from the top is the second string (A), third from the top is the third string (D), and the bottom line is the fourth string (G).

A zero on any of the lines means to play that string unfretted or open. If you see a numeral "1," put your fretting finger on the first fret of whatever string is designated and pick the note. The numbers in italics (1, 2, 3, 4)

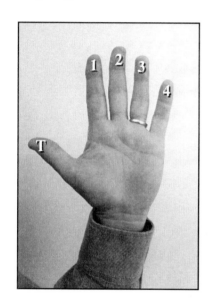

directly above or below the tablature line tell you which fretting hand finger to use to fret a note. You'll see quite a few of these finger notations in the first few songs. After that, if a melody note repeats, we'll leave out the fretting finger designation for the sake of clarity in the music. Eventually we'll leave them out altogether, unless there's an unusual fingering I want to point out, and you'll be able to figure them out for yourself.

In the example below we see the melody and chords to "Camptown Races" shown in standard notation. Below the music staff you'll find the corresponding tablature staff. The first two G notes are played at the fifth fret of the third string. The next note, an E, is played at the second fret of the third string. This is followed by another G. In the next measure, the first note is an A, played on the open second string. Fretting finger numbers are shown in italics below the lyrics and above the tablature staff. We're suddenly swimming in numbers here so don't get confused. Remember that the tablature numbers are on the horizontal lines. Fretting finger numbers are above the lines and shown in italics.

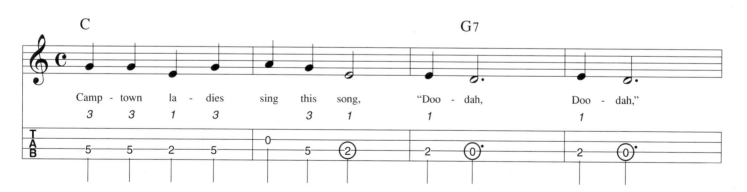

Try "John Hardy," an old time bluegrass standard, in the key of C. For backup rhythm, you can use the chords shown above or look up their closed position counterparts in the Mandolin Chord Dictionary on page 88. Use the simple single down-stroke strum. Listen first and then play along with "John Hardy" on the CD.

For the next several pages we'll be concentrating mainly on chords and rhythm, though tablature for each song's melody is always shown. Concentrate on the chords first, until you can play them all from memory. At that point try to play the melody of each song as shown in the tablature. If you find it too difficult right now, don't worry, we'll study lead playing in depth and you'll be able to come back to all of these songs. Eventually though, you will want to be able to read and play all of the melodies of all the songs and tunes in this book.

John Hardy

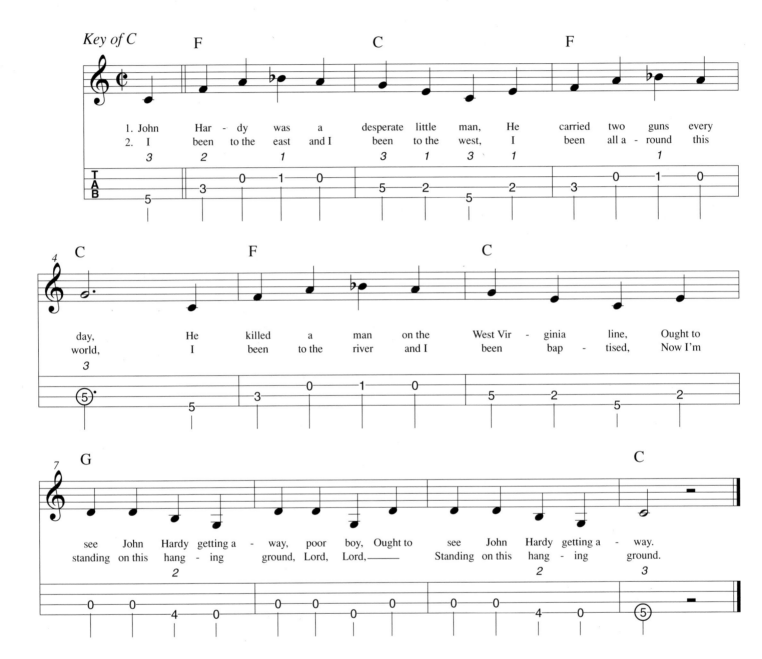

Be a Good Listener

If you want to a good mandolin player, you have to listen to the mandolin being played, both on recordings and live in concert. If you want to become a good bluegrass mandolin player, you need to listen to bluegrass mandolin. Start with Bill Monroe.

Bill Monroe defined bluegrass as a style of music and almost single-handedly defined the role of the mandolin in this, "his" music. It would behoove you to start listening to Bill Monroe right now! His recordings span sixty years but I suggest that you start with some of the earlier material. Check out his pre-bluegrass work with his brother Charlie in the Monroe Brothers and also his early bluegrass from Columbia and Decca. It's of paramount importance to learn from the master of the form. As I write this in early 2004, a wonderful collection of Monroe Brothers and Bill's early bluegrass recordings is available for a great price (under $30.00 for four import CDs!) from JSP Records (JSP 7712). Snap it up if you can find it. JSP also has a similarly priced collection of early Carter Family music, another group whose legend looms large in bluegrass. If you can't locate these CD sets, drop me an e-mail and I'll give you what information I can: info@musixnow.com. Bear Family has four wonderful collections of all of Monroe's recordings with copious notes and informative booklets.

Bill's bluegrass may scare you at first, either because the aggressive singing or instrumental styles are so new to your ears, or it may just be intimidating because it's so fast, so intense, and so good. You may think you'll never be able to do it, but with a little work, you can. There's only one Bill Monroe and you'll never sound just like him, but you can sound like yourself and play your version of bluegrass. Just start listening to Bill and other classic bluegrass musicians and you'll learn what the style is all about and hopefully learn to love the music. As I mentioned, it's intense, and not all that far removed from another great music born in roughly the same time frame: rock and roll. In fact, one of Elvis' first hits was Bill's "Blue Moon of Kentucky." So, get those CDs and start listening.

Will the Circle Be Unbroken

"Will the Circle Be Unbroken" is one of the greatest hits of old time and bluegrass music. This version is in the key of A and the chords are shown below. The ovals in the chord diagrams mean that you should fret two strings with one finger. The A and E are closed chords, the D, which you used above, has open strings. Since the A and E are closed chords, you can move them up or down the fingerboard to make different chords at different frets. For example, you can move the A form "down" or toward the nut, one fret or half step and the new chord will be an A♭. Now go back to the original A position, move it "up" or toward the bridge one fret and the new chord will be a B♭. In the same way, if you move the E form up one fret, the new chord will be an F. Move the F up two more frets and the new chords will be a G.

Be sure to learn the chords and the melody. As you play along with the CD, you can adjust the balance on your amplifier to hear one part or the other. If you're listening with headphones, take one side or the other off. If you're motivated, look up the chords' "bluegrass chop" counterparts in the Mandolin Chord Dictionary on page 88.

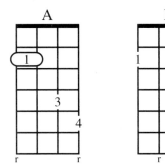
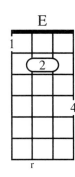

Will the Circle Be Unbroken

Great Big Bad Bluegrass Chop Chords

Now that you've had a little experience with some open-string chords and a few melodies, let's move on to closed position chords, which are really the essence of bluegrass chords and accompaniment.

In my "First Lessons: Mandolin" set, I referred to these types of closed position chords as "Great Big Bad Bluegrass Chop Chords." The name is somewhat tongue-in-cheek because every picker complains at first about how difficult these chords are to make. I don't know if that fact offers any consolation to you but you are not alone and these chords are a rite of passage into bluegrass mandolinhood. We'll use these closed position chords along with a new strumming technique to play bluegrass rhythm.

In a bluegrass band, the mandolinist plays several roles:

1) lead soloist playing melodies,

2) accompanist playing chords,

3) "drummer" playing solid rhythmic backbeats;

4) accompanist playing tasteful background lines and fills behind the vocalist, and

5) babe or dude magnet, as the case may be.

In playing bluegrass rhythm, the mandolinist accomplishes #2 and #3 at the same time supplying accompaniment chords and backbeat rhythm. Before we go any further, listen to a demonstration of "Bluegrass Mandolin Rhythm" and "Bluegrass Chop" on the CD and look at the rhythm diagram below. These chord forms have no open-string notes. They can be moved to different positions up and down the neck to make different chords. The small number to the right of the chord grid tells at which fret number the form should be placed and acts as an anchor point for our fretting fingers. More on that in a minute. In the A and D below, the first finger of your fretting hand should be in fret number four. In the E7, the first finger of your fretting hand should be in fret number six. Try to play along with the CD and learn the new chords.

As you listen to the recorded examples and study the rhythm chart, notice that the mandolin doesn't strum on every beat. Each of the measures in this song has four beats: 1, 2, 3, and 4. The guitar plays bass notes on beats 1 and 3, known as the downbeats. Strums on beats 2 and 4, are known as the backbeats. The mandolin strums on beats 2 and 4, the backbeats, with the guitar strum, and does not play or "rests" on beats 1 and 3. If we had a string bass on the recording, the bass would play its notes on beats 1 and 3, the downbeats, with the guitar bass notes. See the rhythm diagram on page 18.

Altogether it's like a drummer's basic groove in a rock or country band. The drummer "kicks" the bass drum on the downbeats, beats 1 and 3, and plays the snare on the backbeats, 2 and 4. The role of the mandolin is like that of the snare drum and except for accents and special fills, the mandolin always plays on beats 2 and 4 and rests on beats 1 and 3. If you have trouble resting on beats 1 and 3 and fitting in the chops on 2 and 4, try playing a very light click on 1 and 3 just to keep your own rhythm together. You want it to be very light, virtually unheard by anyone else and eventually you'll want to stop playing it altogether. Listen to "More on Chop Chords" on the CD.

Once you can play a few chords and have begun your love affair with lead playing, you'll have a tendency to concentrate more on leads than rhythm. You'll probably think that playing hot and sexy leads is where it's at as far mandolin playing goes. **Wrong! Rhythm is the most important aspect of good mandolin playing.** (Sorry to shout, but I'm passionate on this point.) Speed and flash mean nothing if your rhythm stinks. If you don't groove, no one who plays with you can groove. It's a delicate thing and it really requires your concentration and dedication.

So, how does one develop good mandolin rhythm? Start by recognizing the importance of good rhythm. Then try to define what that means. Listen to CDs by the masters, Monroe, Flatt & Scruggs, Jimmy Martin, Tony Rice, David Grisman, etc. Learn how those bands work and how they groove. Work your way up to playing along with them. You might make up your own jam CD or cassette of favorite cuts by your favorite bands to play along with. Get started right away by playing along with me on the included CD. As you'll hear, good rhythm is more than keeping metronomic time. Jam with other musicians, especially those slightly better than you, whenever you can. (For more info on jamming, see page 86.) Your rhythmic sense will develop over time if you work on it. And remember, you can't possibly put in too much time on rhythm.

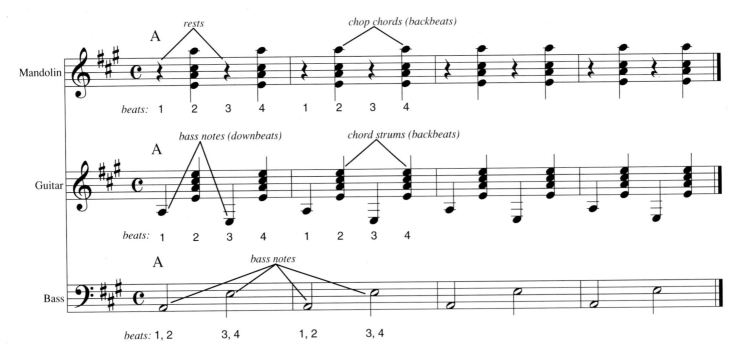

The mandolin strum or "chop," sounds clipped and shouldn't ring like the open-strings chords you previously played. This is to emphasize the backbeats on beats 2 and 4. As you develop as a player, you'll discover that you *can* let the chop ring for varying lengths of time for a range of effects and expression. For now though, concentrate on playing a clipped, but even and controllable chop. To make the chop we need to use closed position chords with no open or ringing strings. We also need to be able to "stop" the ringing of the notes whenever we want. We do it all with our fretting hand. It's as simple as this: hold the chord, strum it, then relax the grip on the chord just enough to stop the sound. Don't lift your fingers off the strings altogether, but rather, pulse your fretting hand.

At first glance, these chords look impossibly difficult. No doubt about it, they are tough. But you **will** be able to play them, it just takes time and practice. The good news is that since these chord forms are in closed (all strings fretted or muted) positions, they are moveable all over the fingerboard. As I mentioned regarding "Will the Circle Be Unbroken," you can learn one form and then move it to eight or more other positions to play that many other chords! For example, move the chop A form up one fret and the new chord is B♭. Move it down one fret from the original A position and the new chord is A♭. Move the closed D up one fret and it becomes D♯. Down one fret from it's original D position and the new chord is D♭. Likewise, move the closed E7 up one fret to F7. Move it down from the original E7 to E♭7.

Look again at the A, D, and E7 chop chords. As you already know, the small number 4 off to the right of the chord grid tells at which fret to make the chord. When you play this A, make sure your first finger, shown with a "1" in the grid, frets the second string at the fourth fret. When you play the chop D, make sure your first finger frets the third string at the fourth fret. When you play the E7, make sure your first finger frets the third string at the sixth fret.

You may have noticed that with both the D and the E7 chords we play three strings instead of four. Can we do that? Yes! Is it legal? Well, mostly. It sounds perfectly appropriate in bluegrass rhythm because it gives a good solid backbeat "chop" sound. You might think that since the mandolin has only four strings to begin with, we should always play every one, but that's not how bluegrass mandolin rhythm has evolved. Of course, you can always substitute a four string chord. It will have a slightly different sound and may require a fretting hand shift.

Remember that the small "x" under string 1 on both the D and E7 tells us to not play that string. The best way is to mute string one with the fleshy part of your fretting hand or finger(s). It may take some hand wiggling at first to find just the right position and pressure. You'll need to work at it until you discover for yourself what gives you the best results. It's of utmost importance in playing rhythm. Go back to the previous version of "Will the Circle Be Unbroken" on page 16 and plug in these closed position chop chords.

East Virginia Blues

Let's learn another song with closed position "chop" chords. "East Virginia Blues" is a traditional bluegrass standard that you should know. It's in the key of E. Look at the chords below. Notice that the first chord, the E, is identical to the D chord you learned in "Will the Circle Be Unbroken," except that it is played two frets higher than the D. Try to start recognizing the shapes of these chords as forms rather than as an "A chord" or a "D chord" since they can be moved up and down the fingerboard to make different chords. I often refer to the A chord below, which you also learned in the last song, as the big daddy chop chord or the "outside" chop chord. I refer to the E (or the D in the last song) as the "inside chop chord" since we don't use string one, but rather, damp or mute it with the side of one of the fretting fingers.

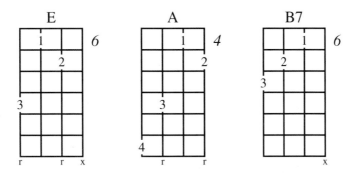

The B7 is new, and as you can see, it has no root note. (No little "r" under the grid.) Can we do this? Yes! Is it legal? Absolutely! That's my story and I'm sticking to it! Both the guitar and the bass are playing chord roots all the time so they won't be missed.

Before we go on to the song, let's look at how the "seventh form" or B7 in this case, relates to the basic major chord that shares its letter name. First, move the A chop chord up two frets on the fingerboard. What chord is it now? If you guessed B, you are correct. See below.

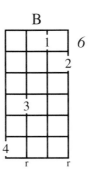

When you have that chord firmly in your head and hands, move your second finger to the third string, seventh fret, and your third finger to the fourth string, eighth fret. It should look like this:

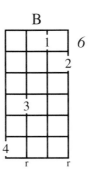

Practice moving back and forth between the B and B7 chords. Then go back down to the A position and practice moving between A and A7. Try similar exercises up and down the fingerboard. In both the B and B7 chop chords the first finger of your fretting hand should be in fret number six.

East Virginia Blues

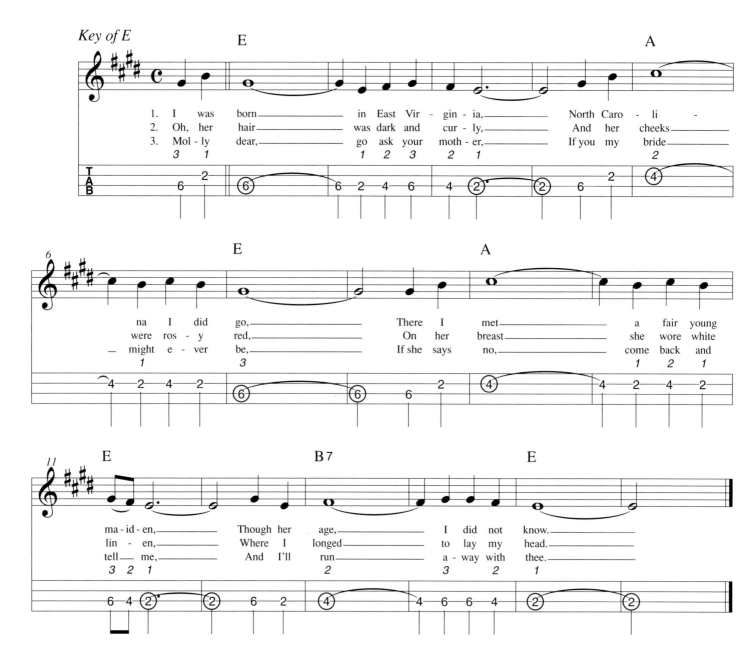

Key of E

```
1. I was born____ in East Vir - gin - ia,____ North Caro - li -
2. Oh, her hair____ was dark and cur - ly,____ And her cheeks____
3. Mol - ly dear,____ go ask your moth - er,____ If you my bride____

na I did go,____ There I met____ a fair young
were ros - y red,____ On her breast____ she wore white
— might e - ver be,____ If she says no,____ come back and

ma - id - en,____ Though her age,____ I did not know.____
lin - en,____ Where I longed____ to lay my head.____
tell__ me,____ And I'll run____ a - way with thee.____
```

Bury Me Beneath the Willow

Here's "Bury Me Beneath the Willow" in the key of D. The chords will be very similar to those in "East Virginia Blues." In fact, they'll be the same chords moved down the fingerboard (down in pitch, toward the nut) by two frets. See below.

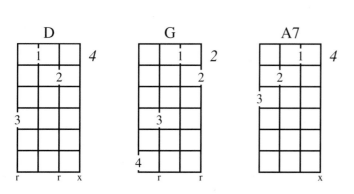

As soon as you try the G chop chord, you'll realize that it's usually easier to move a chord position (and eventually a melody) up the fingerboard than down. As you go up the fingerboard, the frets get smaller; as you go down, they get larger. Your fingers stay the same size. So, the G chop is a bear! Don't expect to be able to play it cleanly in five minutes, even if you're totally comfortable with the B and A chops. It'll take some time and a lot of practice, but it will get better. A good rule of thumb in approaching bluegrass mandolin, or just about anything else for that matter, is to **practice what you don't know, not what you do know.** Work on the things that give you problems, not on the things you already know how to do. Of course your tendency will be to play the things you can play again and again — it's a source of pure joy! But, try to temper that urge with a lust to keep learning and master the things that might be a little weak. Only you can know how much practice a chord, song, or melody needs. I'm not sure that practice makes perfect, but it does make better!

Play through the song and sing along. "Bury Me Beneath the Willow" is a great song and is performed wherever bluegrassers play. As I mentioned before, once you've mastered the chords, try playing the melody, which is shown in both standard notation and tablature. We'll get into playing melodies soon and in a few pages you'll learn about the rules of pick direction, but there's no harm in trying to play a few melodies now.

Gibson "A" model, ca. 1924

Photo by Dix Bruce

Bury Me Beneath the Willow

You've probably noticed that the three chords to "East Virginia Blues," just like the chords on all the other songs you've learned, fit into a "region" on the fingerboard and relate spatially to one another. You should see a pattern emerging between the chords: over one string, up two frets, etc. Together, the three chords make a neat package. Why is this important? Two reasons: Most bluegrass songs have two or three chords and you can move the package up and down the fingerboard and *transpose* "Bury Me Beneath the Willow" to many other keys to accommodate different voice and instrument ranges.

Let's try moving the whole chord package up two frets. For now, don't think about what the names of these chords will be at the new location, just try to visualize how the package looks in your mind's eye. Then move the whole package up and play through the song. If you maintain the relative relationships the chords had in the original key, you should be able to play "Bury Me Beneath the Willow" at the new location without thinking too much about chords or transposing. We'll study transposing a song from one key to another in greater depth later so don't worry if you find this difficult right now. I just wanted to introduce the concept to you so you start thinking about and trying out the process.

This next exercise can strike fear into the hearts of some Bluegrass musicians. *Oh no! we're going to play in the key of A♭!* The reason that the key of A♭ strikes fear is that it is a somewhat unusual key for bluegrass and folk musicians and they tend to avoid learning to play in A♭. Mandolins, fiddles, guitar, and banjos are tuned in such a way as to favor keys like G, D, and A, the so called sharp keys, as well as the key of C. These keys offer a lot of open-string notes and make possible certain techniques and licks. You do have to fret more notes to play a melody in A♭ than you do in A (check out the tablature to "Long Journey Home" on page 25) but there's little difference when you are playing chords. And, as I mentioned above, it's a good idea to be able to play in every key. You'll be a better player.

Long Journey Home

"Long Journey Home" is in the key of A♭. You're already familiar with these chord forms from your second look at "Will the Circle Be Unbroken." For the key of A♭, we'll move these key of A chords down the fingerboard by one fret. If you're brave, try playing the chords without looking at the chord grids below!

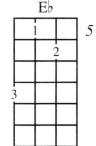

In "East Virginia Blues" we compared the B and B7 chords. Let's do a similar thing with the inside chop chords E♭ and E♭7 to familiarize you with how they are related. Make the E♭ chord shown at left. When you have it firmly in your head and hands, move your second finger to the fourth string, sixth fret. Now move your third finger to the second string sixth fret.

It should look like the chord on the right:

Practice moving back and forth between the E♭ and E♭7 chords. Then move the forms up and down the fingerboard to teach your head and hands how these chords feel.

Back when we were working on "Roll in My Sweet Baby's Arms," I mentioned that keys, and as you'll see, notes and chords, can have two different names. For example, A♯ and B♭ are the same key, note or chord. Ditto with C♯/D♭, D♯/E♭, F♯/G♭, G♯/A♭. These are *enharmonic* names for the same note or chord. So, E♭ is also D♯, A♭ is G♯, A♯ is B♭, whether we're talking about notes, chords, or keys. When you play "Long Journey Home" in the key of A♭, you're also playing it in the key of G♯. When you play an A♭ chord or note, you're also playing a G♯ chord or note.

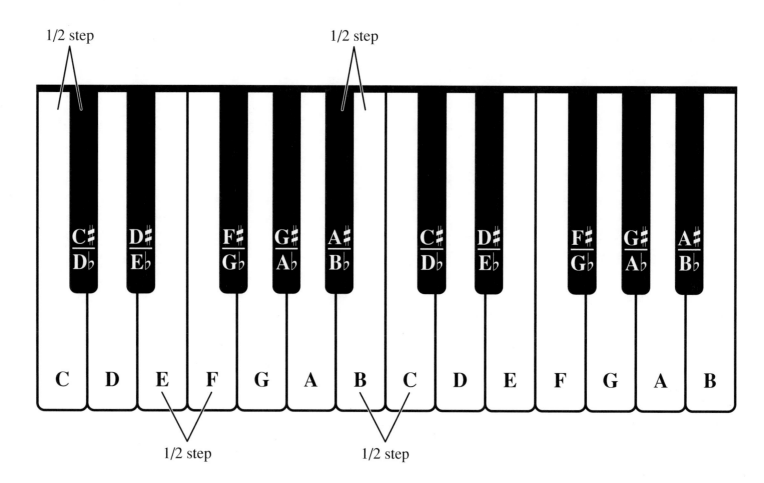

The white keys have single letter names: A, B, C, etc. The black keys have enharmonic names: A♯/B♭, C♯/D♭, D♯/E♭, etc. You can refer to the black keys by either of the names but theoretically it's best to consider the context in deciding whether it's an A♯ or a B♭. Without getting too deeply into this, let's say you start out on a B note and lower or "flat" the B by one half step. You'd call the new note "B♭" not "A♯." If you start with an A note and raise or "sharp" it by one half step, the new note would be "A♯" and not "B♭." So context matters and gives us more information about a note or chord. If you're playing in a **sharp key,** G, D, A, E, B, enharmonic notes in those keys are most correctly described with sharps: F♯, C♯, G♯, etc. If you're playing in a *flat key,* F, B♭, E♭, A♭, D♭, enharmonic notes in those keys are most correctly described with flats: B♭, E♭, A♭, D♭, etc. The key of C is neither sharp nor flat since there are no sharp or flat notes in the C major scale: C, D, E, F, G, A, B. While playing in A♭, B♭, E♭, and D♭ is rare in bluegrass, playing in the key of B is quite common. Eventually you should try moving "Long Journey Home" and "All the Good Times" to the key of B. We'll work with transposing in the "Modulation & Transposing" section on page 61.

Long Journey Home

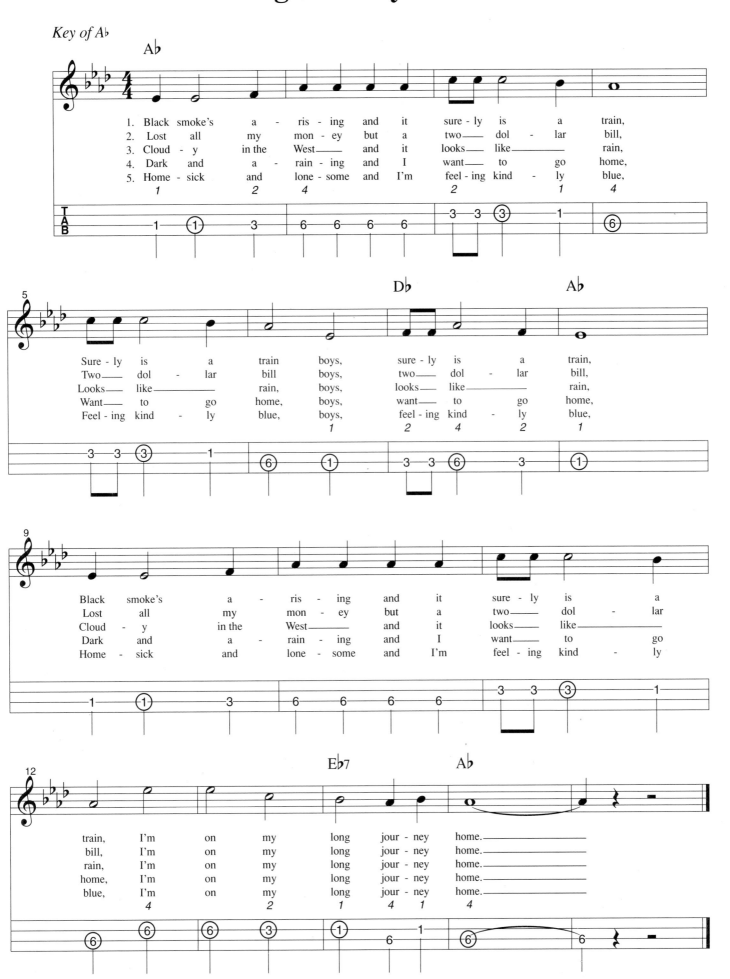

All the Good Times are Past and Gone

"All the Good Times are Past and Gone" is a waltz, so our rhythmic framework will be slightly different than we've had so far. Previously our rhythmic scheme was based on four beats to a measure. We rest on beats one and three and play chops on beats two and four. This is often described as "playing in four" and we'd count it "one-two-three-four."

4/4 mandolin rhythm:

In a waltz, our rhythmic scheme is based on three beats to a measure. Here we'll rest on beat one and chop chords on beats two and three. This is often described as "playing in three" and we'd count it "one-two-three." Listen to example "3/4 Rhythm" on the CD.

3/4 mandolin rhythm:

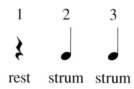

"All the Good Times are Past and Gone" is written here in another scary key: B♭. Of course it's silly for me to call it scary. It won't scare you—you've already played in a much scarier key—A♭. The chords are shown below, but before you look at them, try playing "All the Good Times" by just moving the whole package of A chords up one fret.

When you do look at the chord grids below, you'll see how much they look like the chords in the key of A, only a fret higher on the fingerboard.

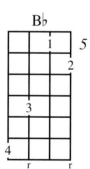 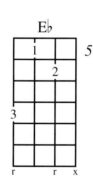 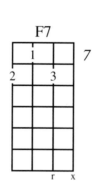

It's very important that you practice playing these rhythm chords with the bluegrass chop. You want to develop it so that it's even in time and volume. You also want to be able to do it with any set of chords in any key. It won't come without a lot of work, a lot of listening, and a lot more work. As I said before, once you recognize these chord forms and can play them here and there, you might feel a tendency to slack off and not practice your rhythm. Fight that tendency! As you move on to solos and melodies, be sure to spend a healthy part of your daily practice sessions on chords and rhythm. Play along with my accompanying CD and with other CDs too. Keep in mind that as a mandolin player in a bluegrass band, you'll be playing rhythm about three quarters of the time, if not more. So, it has to be good. The others in the band will be depending on you for rhythmic and harmonic structure.

All the Good Times are Past and Gone

Key of B♭

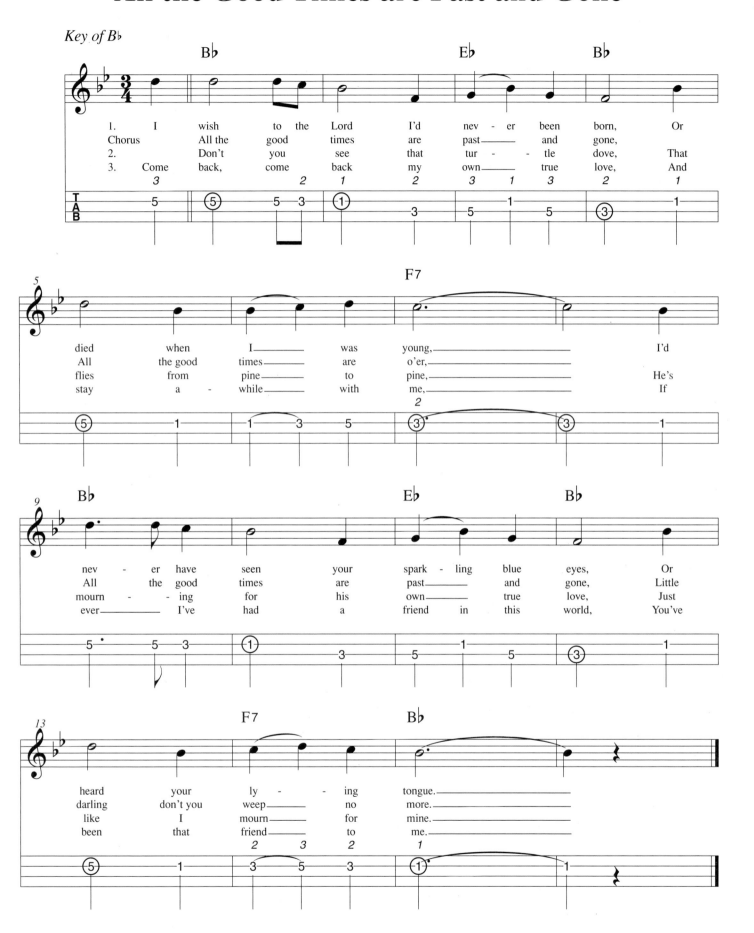

27

Aura Lee & First Leads

I can sense it, your picking fingers are getting itchy to learn more leads and solos. The next few songs are designed to officially get you playing single note melodies. At first they'll be quite simple, not all that bluegrassy, mostly quarter notes played with all down strokes. Next we'll add in eighth notes, which will require up and down picking. Once you're comfortable playing a variety of simple melodies, we'll get into some more challenging and more specifically bluegrass solos.

As with "John Hardy," on "Aura Lee" we'll play all of the notes in the melody with single down-strokes of the pick. That's because all of the notes in "Aura Lee" are quarter notes or longer. Look at the diagram below which identifies quarter, half and whole notes.

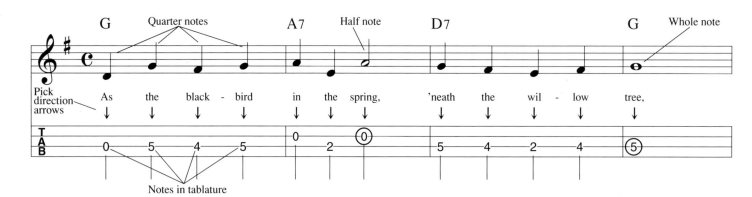

Quarter notes look like a filled in circle with a stem, placed on a line or space of the staff. Half notes look like an open circle with a stem and wholes notes look like an open circle without a stem. In 4/4 time, quarter notes are played and allowed to sound for one beat. Half notes are played and allowed to sound for two beats. Whole notes are played and allowed to sound for four beats. A dot after a note (called an *augmentation* dot) adds one half of the value to that note. So, a dotted half gets three beats, a dotted quarter gets one and one half beats.

Our basic rule of thumb (pun totally unintended) for pick direction is this: if the length of the note is quarter or longer (half note or whole note) we play it with a down-stroke of the pick. Pick direction is noted between the staves with down (↓) or up (↑) arrows. For now, all the notes will be played with down-strokes. It will get more complicated when we get to eighth notes.

"Aura Lee" is a beautiful old song that was given new lyrics in the late 1950s and became one of Elvis Presley's biggest hits as "Love Me Tender." Listen to the recording on the CD and play along, first chords, then melody. You've already worked with most of the chords: G, A7, and B7. The D7 is shown below and it's just like one of the other seventh forms you've had. Em ("E minor") introduces a new kind of chord, the *minor*. Once you can play the first form at the fourth fret, try the alternate Em chord lower on the fingerboard. The difficulty with this form is that your hand will have to jump from the higher B7 position to the lower Em. Still it's good to know as many forms of a given chord as possible. All the chords are listed alphabetically in the back of this book. As you play rhythm on this slow ballad in 4/4, you may find it helpful to tap your foot on beats one and three as you play rhythm chords on beats two and four.

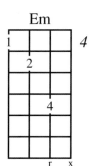
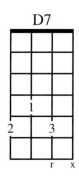
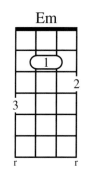

Once you're comfortable playing both the lead and rhythm to "Aura Lee," go back and try playing the melodies to all the previous tunes. As we progress technically, you'll be coming back to these basic tunes again and again to practice new concepts.

28

Aura Lee

Fiddle Tunes & Eighth Notes

Every bluegrass mandolin player needs to know some fiddle tunes. "Old Joe Clark" is a good place to start. The following version of the tune is simplified: I took out many of the eighth notes but left enough to give you an introduction into the down and up picking that eighth notes require. The example below shows what eighth notes look like in both standard notation and tablature. Eighth notes look a lot like quarter notes except that they have a little flag attached to the stem. When eighth notes appear in a series, they are often beamed.

In 4/4 or 3/4 time, a quarter note is held for one beat, a half note is held for two beats, and a whole note is held for four beats. An eighth note has one half the value of a quarter and gets one half beat. Two eighth notes fit into the time of one quarter note, so two eighth notes are played over one beat. The important consideration in pick direction is to determine **where** on the beat and in the measure a note falls.

In the example below, I've diagrammed a simple melody to show how mixed note values are counted. In the first measure we have all quarters counted "one, two, three, four." In the second measure we have mixed quarters and a half note counted "one, two, three, (four)." We'd "think" beat four but wouldn't play it. Rather, we'd let the note from beat three ring over beat four. Measure three, with mixed eighth and quarter notes, is where it gets interesting. It's counted like this: "one and, two and, three, four" with plus signs representing the "ands." These count numbers are shown immediately below the notes in bold italics. We'll rarely show count numbers like these in the music. Usually when you see numbers they'll refer to picking finger numbers. Just remember that if you see bold italic numbers, they'll refer to beat counts.

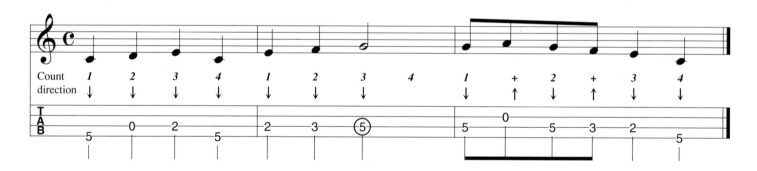

Our basic rule for pick direction is this: if the length of the note is quarter or longer (half note or whole note) we play it with a down-stroke of the pick. Eighth notes will be played with either a down or an up stroke depending upon where on the beat the eighth note occurs. Here's the rule pertaining to eighth notes: If an eighth note falls on beat one, two, three, or four, play it with a down-stroke of the pick. If it falls on any of the "ands," play it with an upstroke. These are noted in the diagram above with down (↓) or up (↑) arrows. As the music gets more advanced, you'll run into exceptions and addenda to this rule. Also, when you get to be an advanced player, you can pick in any direction you want. This rule is to get you started and give you a way of analyzing music to determine how to play it efficiently. Listen to "Pick Direction" on the CD.

"Old Joe Clark" includes a line of down (↓) and up (↑) arrows to show pick direction. You won't see them in every measure, just where you might need them to get going. Eventually you won't need them at all.

Directly below the arrows are more numbers. Notice that they are in italic text (but not bold-italic). These numbers represent fretting finger numbers, 1 though 4, just like in the chord grids you've already seen and used. Again, you won't find finger numbers under every note, just enough to get your hand positioned correctly.

"Old Joe Clark" also has measure numbers and repeats. Measure numbers make it easy for us to identify a measure in the music. You'll notice the first measure number, 5, above the treble clef sign in staff two. That measure is the fifth full measure. As a shorthand we'll use "m5" to mean "measure five" in the text.

In m8 you'll see a backward-facing repeat mark consisting of double dots, a thin line and a thick line on the right side of the measure. When you see this repeat mark, go back to the previous forward-facing repeat mark (thick line on left, thin line in the middle, double dots on the right), in this case in m1, and play the whole section enclosed by the forward and backward repeat marks, m1-m8, again. Then go on to the next part, which also has repeat marks enclosing the section, m9-m16, and play through it twice. By the way, the forward repeat at the beginning isn't absolutely necessary. If the first backward repeat you see in a tune has no corresponding forward repeat in a previous measure, it means to repeat from the top. You only really need a forward repeat if there are any measures (or partial measures) that are not part of the repeated section (like a pickup, for instance). This only applies to the first backward repeat of a tune. Any repeat after the first one *does* require a forward repeat (because you have to know how far to go back!).

One last thing about repeat marks, if a backward repeat and a forward repeat fall on consecutive measures within the same line, they will look like this:

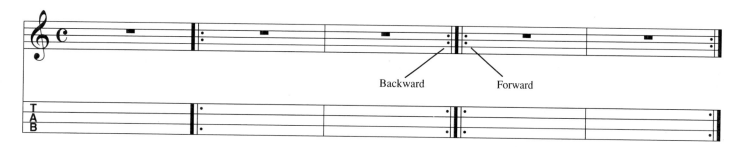

Be sure to practice the chords to the following tunes as you learn the melodies. Use the chop chords you've already learned. Look back in the text or consult the Chord Dictionary on page 88 if you need to.

31

Old Joe Clark

32

Ragtime Annie

"Ragtime Annie" also has measure numbers and first and second endings. You'll notice the first one, "5," above the treble clef sign in staff two. That tells us that this is the fifth full measure. We don't count the pickup measure, but start counting with the first full measure.

We also have a new kind of repeat: a *first ending* (found in m8) and a *second ending* (found in m9). This tells us that when we come to the backward-repeat symbol in m8, we go back to the forward-repeat symbol after the pickup measure (as we would with a regular repeat). The difference is that after we play m7 the second time, we skip over m8, and instead play m9. From there, we procede on to m10 and go from there.

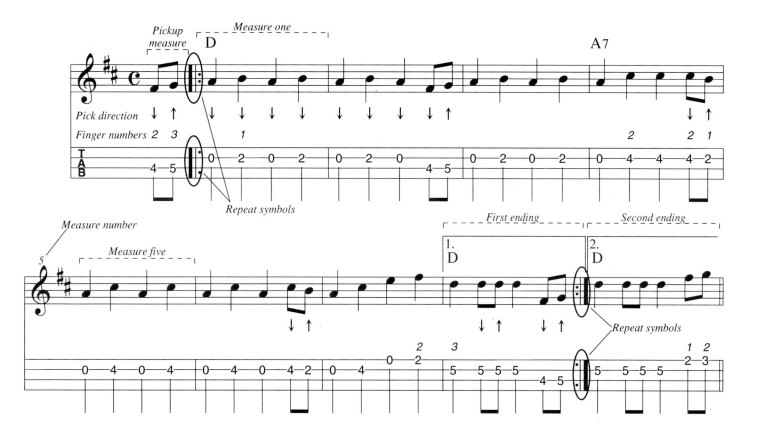

Banjo-mandolins

Photo by Dix Bruce

Ragtime Annie

Liberty

"Liberty" has even more eighth notes. Pay attention to the arrows and fretting finger numbers and you'll be fine.

Liberty

35

Bluegrass Solos

Bluegrass mandolinists don't just play a melody exactly as written or sung. They tend to add notes that embellish a straight melody to make it sound more "bluegrassy." Let's look at the standard "Nine Pound Hammer," first with straight melody and then the versions with some notes added. Bill Monroe used this technique extensively in the Monroe Brothers with his brother Charlie and it forms the basis of Monroe's, and ultimately bluegrass mandolin's, style. We won't try to play it quite as fast as Bill, at least not yet!

Nine Pound Hammer
basic version

36

For the next version of "Nine Pound Hammer," I added a lot of eighth notes. They're especially noticeable in place of the longer notes as on lyrics like the second syllable of "ham-mer." If you play the straight melody, the sound kind of dies out, but with the constant eighth notes, it makes a complete solo. You may find it difficult to sustain the continual up and down picking on the eighth notes at first. Just play the solo slowly until your hands gain strength and stamina. Be sure to start listening to Bill Monroe's Monroe Brothers recordings.

Nine Pound Hammer

solo

Crawdad Song

We'll put together a solo for "Crawdad Song" the same way. Learn the basic melody below and then the solo which is based on it.

Crawdad Song
basic version

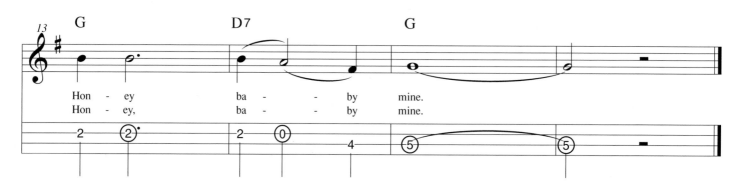

Crawdad Song

solo

Fretting-hand Techniques: Slides, Hammers, Pulls

Bluegrass mandolinists use a variety of fretting and picking techniques in composing solos and leads. We'll look at three of the essentials involving the fretting hand: slides, hammers, and pulls. Let's look at slides first.

Normally we fret and a note and pick it. With a "slide" we fret a note a fret or two below or above our target note and quickly slide to the target note. Listen to the "Slides Example" on the CD. The difficulty with this, and all the fretting-hand techniques, is in keeping the note sounding during the slide. It just takes practice.

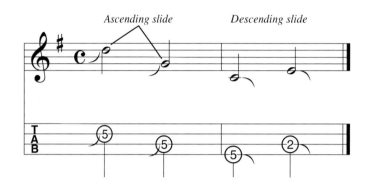

Slides are noted in the music with a small curved line into the target note or tablature number. This curved line looks like a tie or slur. In this book you'll also see a small "s" between the standard notation and the tablature to signify a slide. If there are several slides in a row, as in the exercise below, we'll only identify the first of the series unless it is not obvious.

We can slide into a note from below or above it. In this book, an ascending slide will be shown with a small curved line starting below and ending at our target note. A descending slide will be shown with a small curved line starting above and ending at the target note. Ascending slides are more common in bluegrass music and slightly easier to control than descending slides. See the examples below.

Unless it's specified, it's up to you where you begin your slides. In the exercise below, I suggest that you slide up from two frets below the target notes on ascending slides. On descending slides, begin on the note shown and slide down two frets.

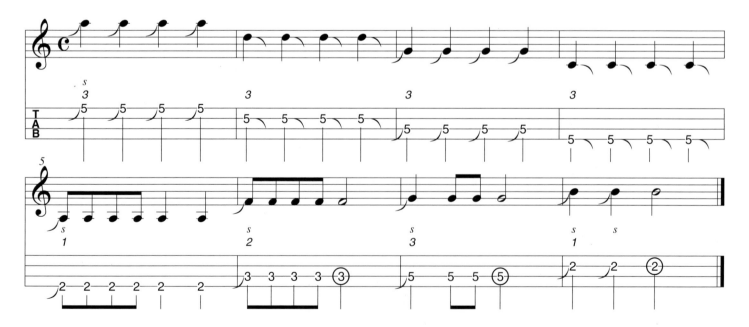

To play a *hammer* or *hammer-on*, first play a note, and while it is ringing, quickly fret another higher note so that the second note sounds without a second pick stroke. As with the slide, the difficulty is in getting a robust second note without muting the string and the sound.

A *pull* or *pull-off* is the opposite of a hammer. First play a fretted note, and while it's ringing, quickly pull off the fretting finger to sound a lower fretted or open-string note. You can use the finger you are pulling off to pluck the new note. Again, the second note should sound without a second pick stroke.

Both hammers and pulls are shown in the standard notation with slurs. A small *"h"* will signify a hammer; a small *"p"* will signify a pull. Often both the starting and the target notes will be connected with the slur. If not, you'll usually be starting from or ending on an open string.

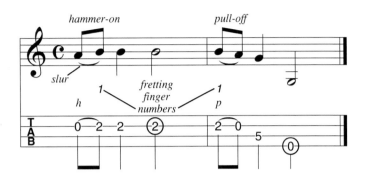

Hammers and pulls can affect pick direction, as you can see in the exercise below. For example, in m1 below we have several eighth notes. We play the first with a down pick, the second is played by the hammer with no pick stroke at all. The third eighth note would then be played with a down pick. If you get confused, remember that if the note falls on beat 1, 2, 3, or 4, we play it with a down pick, if the note falls between those beats or on an "and," play it with an up pick.

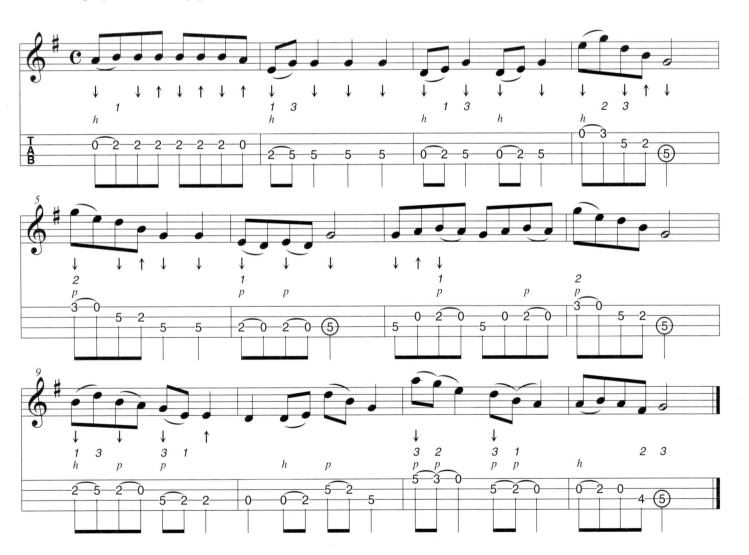

41

When the Saints Go Marching In

"When the Saints Go Marching In," a standard in both country and jazz music, recorded by the Monroe Brothers and Flatt & Scruggs among others, combines several slides, hammers and pulls.

When the Saints Go Marching In

solo

Key of G

Double Stops

As I mentioned before, mandolinists take a basic melody and "bluegrass-ize" it, usually by adding eighth notes but also by adding hammers, slides, and pull-offs. Below is a simple melody version of "Somebody Touched Me" followed by an embellished, more bluegrass sounding version with added eighth notes, slides, hammers, and something new: *double stops.*

Technically speaking, to play a double stop we fret ("stop") and play two notes, usually on two adjacent strings, at the same time. In bluegrass we can refer to any combination of two different notes as a "double stop." They can be fretted, open or a combination of both. A double stop is kind of like a junior chord, and it's treated just like a single note. We get the double stop technique from fiddlers who also play lots of them. You'll find our first double stops in m13 of the solo to "Somebody Touched Me," shown after the simple version directly below. Learn the simple melody before you go on to the solo.

Lyon & Healy style "B" mandolins

Somebody Touched Me

basic version

Key of A

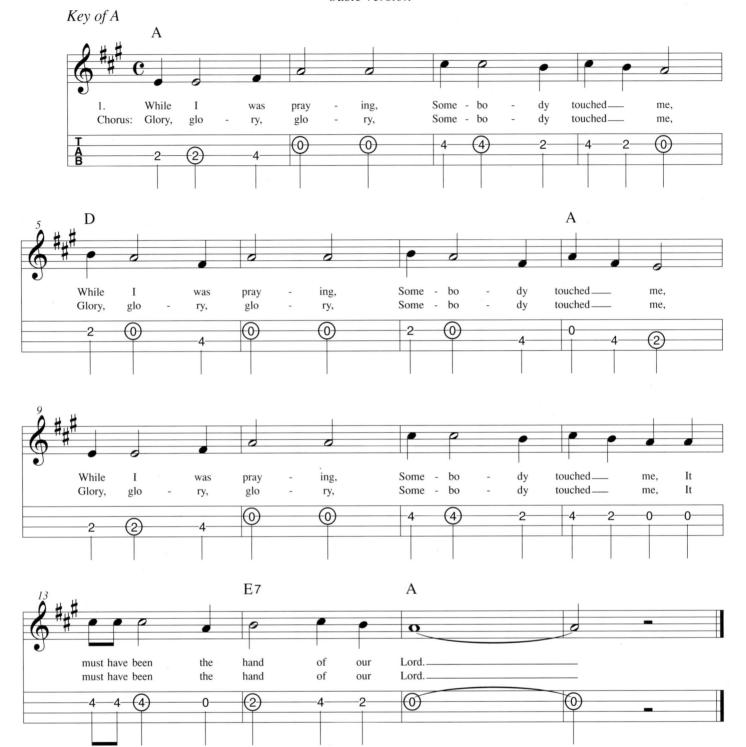

Somebody Touched Me

solo

Key of A

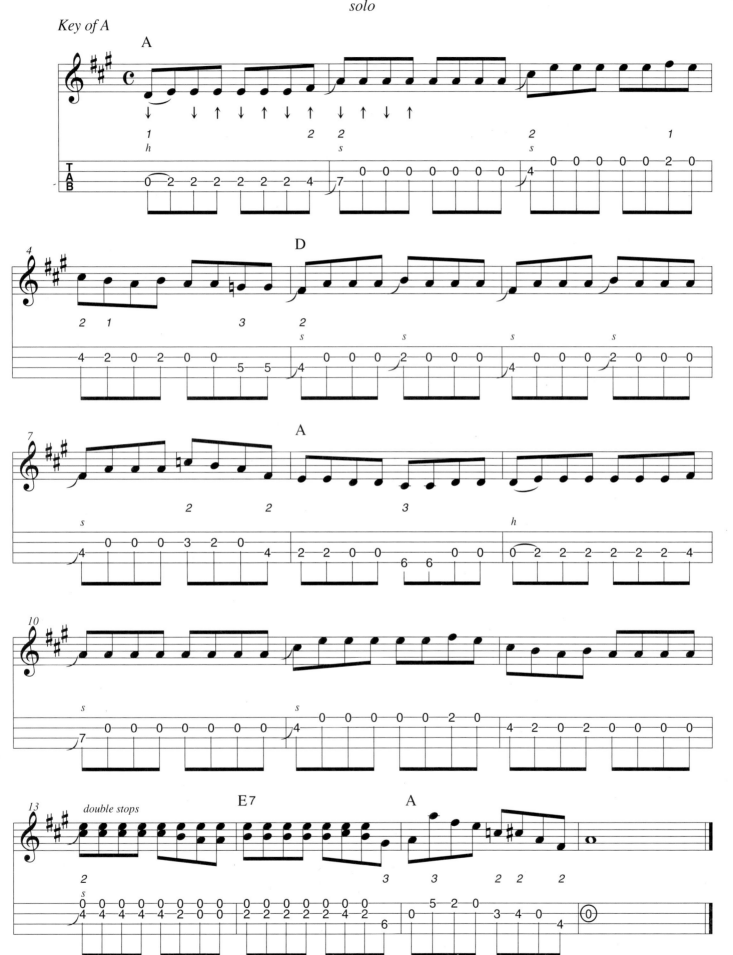

More Double Stops: Will the Circle Be Unbroken

Let's try another solo with more slides and lots of double stops. You've already worked with "Will the Circle Be Unbroken" (page 16) so it should be somewhat familiar to you. This solo makes use of the open first and second strings almost as drones to make the most of the double stops. That means you'll only have to fret one of the two notes of the double stop. As usual, the arrows will remind you about pick direction, the numbers tell you which fretting hand fingers to use, the small *"s"* denotes a slide.

Will the Circle Be Unbroken
solo

Double stops are often made using two fretted notes on two adjacent strings. Here's a two measure substitution for m5 & m6 (under the D chord) which requires you to fret both notes. To tell you the truth, the original doesn't quite fit with the chord there: the open first string E is not part of the D chord. But, in that solo, it works well enough.

Since you'll be fretting two notes, you'll see two stacked fretting finger numbers below. The upper number refers to the higher pitched note, the lower refers to the lower pitched note. Plug these substitute measures into the solo.

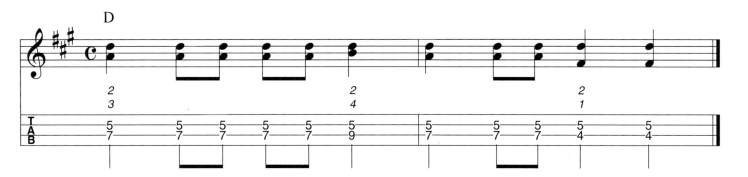

Here's a challenging new version of "Bury Me Beneath the Willow" in the key of C with double stops. You'll have to fret both notes to make most of these double stops. Below is a variation for measures five and six. It's a little more work than the original, but it's nice.

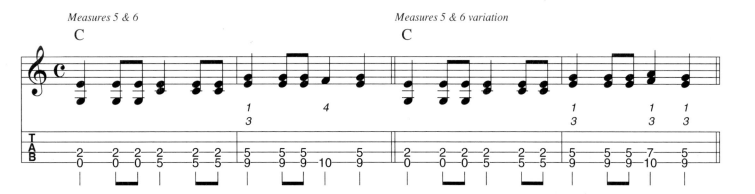

Photos by Dix Bruce

Martin mandolin, "Style 20"   *Gibson "A" mandolin*

47

Bury Me Beneath the Willow

solo

Key of C

Transitions Back Into Rhythm

As you listen to bluegrass mandolinists play solos like those you are learning, you'll notice that the solos don't always end as definitively as they are written here. Usually the solos trail off as the player makes the transition back into playing rhythm chords. Here's an example. Below you'll see the last two measures of the "Bury Me Beneath the Willow" double stop solo. As written, the solo ends on a whole note double stop. This is officially the end of the solo and the next section of the song, whether it's vocal or another instrumental, would begin after this measure.

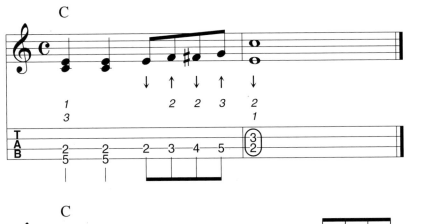

However, the mandolin player, or any soloist for that matter, will usually keep on playing and these notes will overlap the next section and eventually return to playing rhythm. See below.

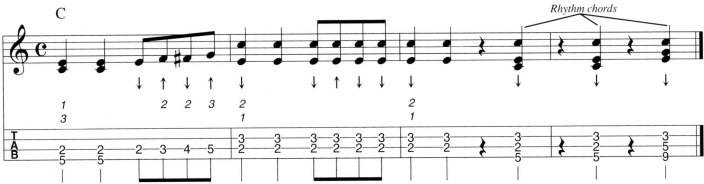

The length of these "solo extensions" depends upon the soloist. It's important that you taper off the volume of whatever you play so the singer or next instrumentalist knows when to come back in. If there's confusion, just keep playing until the singer or instrumentalist starts the next section. Listen to "Solo Endings" on the CD. Let's look at another solo extension.

Here's the last two measures of "Somebody Touched Me." Instead of the whole note, let's repeat the next to last measure a few times as a transition.

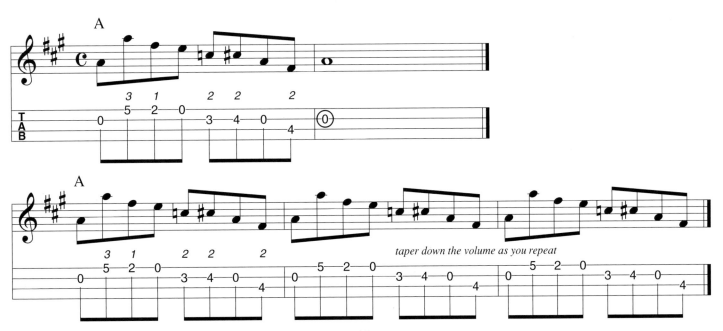

On the solo to "When the Saints Go Marching In" or "Crawdad Song," simply repeat the next to last measure. If the last measure of the solo is a whole note, convert it into four quarter notes, eight eighth notes, or a combination of quarter and eighths. I wrote all the solos in this book with definite endings because I thought it important that you get the feel for the *actual* length of each individual solo. As you work through them, keep in mind that in performance you can extend them in order to build a transition to the next section, where you'll most likely return to rhythm playing and accompanying the singer or another soloist. Listen to players you admire for transition ideas and make up your own.

Right-hand Technique: Tremolo

With a bow, a violinist can extend a note indefinitely. Mandolinists use *tremolo*. On "When the Saints Go Marching In," Nine Pound Hammer," and "Somebody Touched Me," we played a series of eighth notes to extend melody notes and keep the sound going. If we play even more notes in the same period of time to make a denser, more robust and continuous sound, it's called tremolo. Tremolo is a beautifully expressive technique and a must for the mandolinist to master. At its best, tremolo is a smooth, seamless, continuous up-and-down picking of the strings that sounds like one sustained note. It allows the mandolinist to play beautifully legato (extended) passages and is a wonderful dynamic tool when played at different speeds and intensities. For my money, David Grisman is the king of tremolo. He uses it in many different ways to infuse his playing with soul and emotion. Listen to how he does it.

It takes a fair amount of work to master tremolo, so be patient. With tremolo, we're going to fit about twice as many notes into one measure as we have in a typical measure from one of these songs. See the excerpt below.

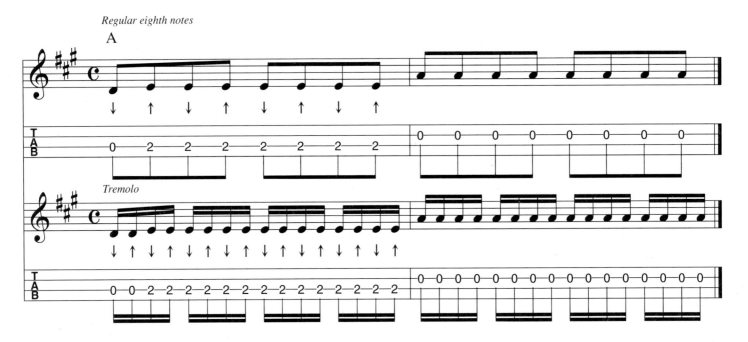

Above I said that we'll be fitting "about twice as many notes" into a measure. I say that because it doesn't have to be exact. Basically we want to get the up and down tremolo "buzz" going and then we'll float melody notes on top of it. The exact number and speed of the notes will depend upon your artistic input. For now though, shoot for sixteenth notes as in the example above. You can practice tremolo on any of the basic songs we've worked on thus far, though you'll have the most luck with those melodies that have longer notes, like quarters, halfs, and whole notes. Listen to the "Tremolo Example" on the CD and then try playing tremolo on "Banks of the Ohio." We won't tremolo every note, only those longer than quarters. I've marked these notes with a slash. When you feel comfortable with your basic tremolo, look back at previous songs and see where you might fit tremolo into them. "Aura Lee" (page 29) is a good one to tremolo all the way through.

50

Banks of the Ohio

solo with tremolo

Down in the Willow Garden

Once you get the tremolo "buzz" going, it can sometimes be difficult to get out of it and play single notes again. "Down in the Willow Garden" will give you practice starting and stopping your tremolo. As with all these songs and exercises, start slowly and build up your speed. Go for an even, smooth feel. You won't find any fretting finger numbers or pick directions in the music. By now you should be able to figure them out yourself by drawing on what you've learned in the previous songs.

Down in the Willow Garden

solo with tremolo

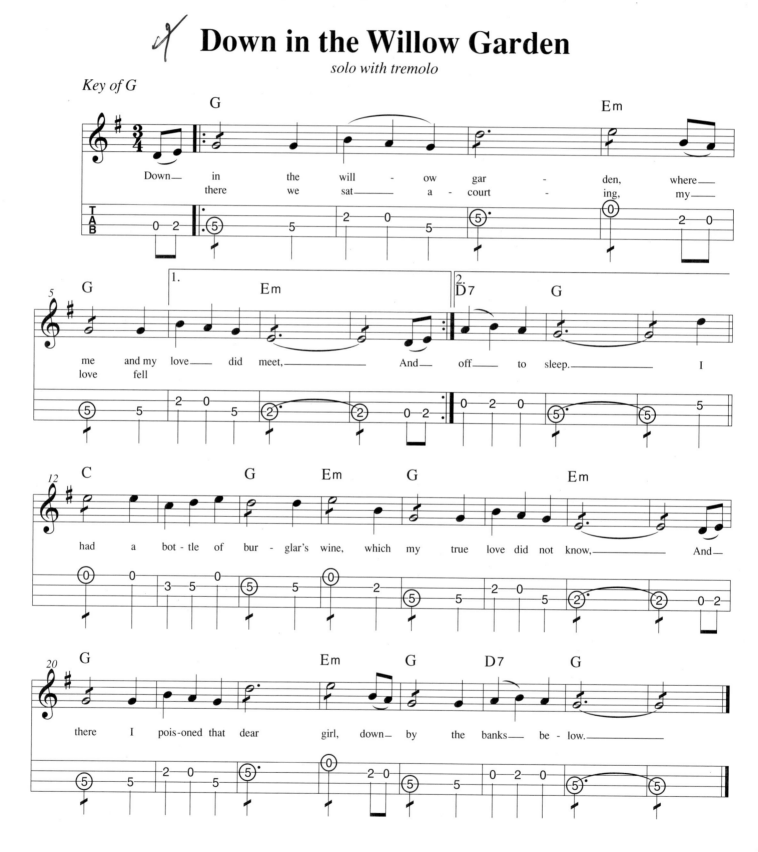

Pass Me Not

This "Pass Me Not" solo combines tremolo and double stops. It'll be a challenge for most of you intermediate pickers. Not only do you have to fret two notes at once, up the neck, you also have to move in and out of tremolo to play both the tremoloed notes and the single note melodic passages. Fretting finger numbers are back: top number, higher note; bottom number, lower note. I didn't mark this one with tremolo slashes since you need to start determining where and when to tremolo on your own. I suggest that you tremolo everything except the eighth notes. Don't worry about pick directions. For simplicity's sake play everything that's not a tremolo (eighth notes) with a down-stroke.

Pass Me Not

solo with double-stops and tremolo

Playing Backup

In addition to playing chord rhythm and lead solos, mandolinists in bluegrass bands often play backup lines behind the vocal and occasionally behind another soloist. These lines need to be subtle, supportive, and complement whatever is the dominant musical event at that time, usually the vocal. Let me say that again: **these lines need to be subtle, supportive, and complement whatever is the dominant musical event at that time, usually the vocal.** Whatever you do, you don't want to draw attention away from the vocal or compete with it in any way, melodically or volume-wise. You'll develop the skill over time and it's helpful to listen to how other mandolinists backup vocalists.

Be sure to ask vocalists you backup if they like your backup. They may find it difficult to sing with your lines. If that's the case, pull back, play less. You don't always have to play backup, a little goes a long way. If in doubt, leave it out. Your choice of what to play to backup a vocalist is pretty much unlimited. We'll explore a some different approaches. Before we get into that, let's review what we already discussed about rhythm roles in a bluegrass band.

Let's assume that our song is in 4/4 with four beats to the measure. (If we had a waltz, it would be in 3/4 with three beats to the measure. For you sticklers: the waltz might also be in 6/8 and we'd think of that as consisting of two times 3/4. In a waltz, the mandolin rests on beat one, strums on beats two and three.) The guitar plays bass notes on beats 1 and 3, or the "downbeats," strums on beats 2 and 4, or the "backbeats." The mandolin strums or chops on beats 2 and 4, the backbeats, with the guitar strum, and does not play or "rests" on beats 1 and 3. The bass would play its notes on beats 1 and 3, the downbeats, with the guitar bass notes. Altogether it's like a drummer's basic groove in a rock or country band. The drummer kicks the bass drum on the downbeats, beats 1 and 3, and hits the snare on the backbeats, 2 and 4. The role of the mandolin is like that of the snare drum and except for accents and special fills, the mandolin always plays on beats 2 and 4, rests on beats 1 and 3. Review the rhythm chart on page 26.

If the mandolin player stops being the snare drummer in order to play backup, the absence of the backbeats can leave a noticeable hole in the rhythm. In a typical five piece bluegrass band (mandolin, guitar, bass, fiddle, and banjo), either the fiddler or banjo player will step in and play backbeat chops (on beats two and four in 4/4 time, or beats two and three in 3/4 time) while the mandolinist is playing a solo or backup. So, before you drop out of the rhythm section, make sure someone else will take up your slack. You wouldn't necessarily ALWAYS have to have the backbeats present on EVERY song, but realize that your backbeat chop is a large part of the groove of the band and your audience depends upon it. Most good fiddlers and banjo players know this and will step up to the plate. If not, discuss it with them and divvy up the backbeat duties.

Many songs in the bluegrass and old-time repertoire are written around a "call and response" structure. These are songs like "Banks of the Ohio," "East Virginia Blues," and "Nine Pound Hammer" where a vocal phrase is sung and followed by a space. Sometimes a note is held during this space. Then the next vocal phrase is sung followed by the next space. A mandolinist can fill these spaces with little licks and phrases and supply a backup part that enhances the vocal and the band performance overall. The vocal is the "call," the backup in the space is called "the response."

I've written out "A Beautiful Life" with four staves instead of the usual two. The top staff shows the melody in standard notation with chords and lyrics. The second staff down is the usual tablature staff of the melody. Under that is the response backup part in standard notation. Below that is the response backup part in tablature. It's a lot to put on a page but it's important that you see how the lead and backup inter-relate. If you have trouble following the correct staff through the whole piece, use a yellow highlighter at the beginning of each backup staff. You can either go back to light chops when you're not playing single or simply lay out and rest. The last staff is blank. Fill it out yourself with appropriate licks from the previous measures or, better yet, make up your own backup licks!

This page has been left blank
to avoid awkward page turns.

A Beautiful Life

backup

Key of G

Wm. Golden, P.D.

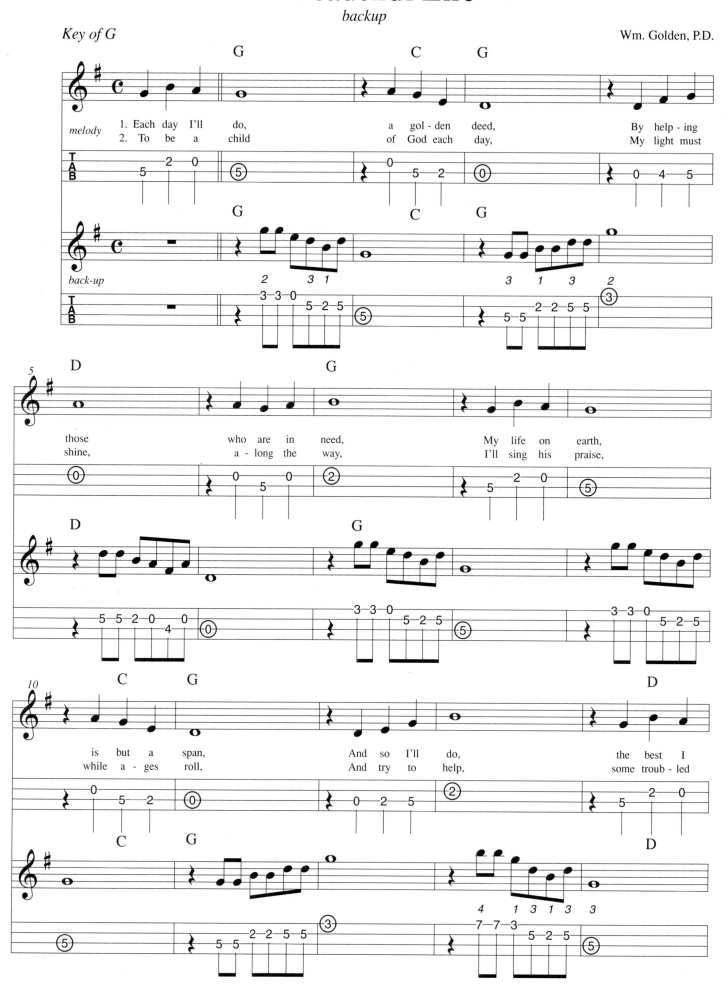

Let's look at a similar "call and response" song with back up, "New River Train." The back up licks are similar to those played by Bill Monroe on the Monroe Brothers recording of this song.

New River Train

"call and response" backup

58

Wash of Notes Backup

Another way of backing up is to play a wash of notes behind the vocal. This arrangement of "In the Pines" demonstrates a type of single-string backup in the first part, and then a double-stop tremolo for the second part. We're not playing the melody here, but a continuous line that we hope will complement the vocal. The two stacked numbers are suggested fretting finger numbers for double stops. The top number tells what finger to use for the upper note, the bottom number for the lower.

You can play this backup part as is or use the single string approach behind the verses, the double-stop tremolo behind the choruses. As always, try to come up with your own ideas. Listening to how other mandolinists backup singers will help you hear what works and what doesn't. Take their best ideas and make them a part of your playing.

The melody to "In the Pines," with all its long notes, is a natural for tremolo.

Dobro® resonator mandolin ca. 1934

Photos by Dix Bruce

National Silver Mandolin, "Style 1"

In the Pines

backup

Modulation & Transposing

One of the great things about the mandolin is that changing keys and transposing are relatively easy because of the way it is tuned. You've already seen how we can move a set of chords up or down the fingerboard to a new key. It's almost as easy to move melodies around in the same way. Why would we want to do this? Because different people play and sing songs in different keys to accommodate their voices or their specific instrument. For example, I might sing "In the Pines" in the key of D while someone with a lower voice might prefer the key of B♭ or someone with a higher voice might prefer the key of F. If you're a bluegrass guitarist, you can slap your capo on the neck, move it up and down the fingerboard, play the same chords but end up in a different key. Mandolinists rarely use capos because once you get the hang of transposing, or moving melodies from one key to another, it's a pretty easy thing to do.

We'll look at two types of transposing, from string to string, kind of across the fingerboard and then from fret to fret, up and down the fingerboard.

Play through the first version of "Lonesome Valley" below in the key of G. The solo (which is closely based on the melody) has both open and fretted strings, and all the notes are on strings two and three. Pay close attention to the suggested fretting hand fingers and memorize this solo before you go on. As you're memorizing, try to picture in your mind the shapes your fretting hand makes as you play through the solo. Try playing it with your eyes closed. When you can do that, you're ready to move on to solo number two.

Gibson Lloyd Load F-5 mandolin

Krishot mandolin

Photos by Dix Bruce

61

Lonesome Valley

basic version in the key of G

Here's where it gets amazing. Let's move the whole melody over one string. Instead of starting on the open third string, your first note will be on the open second string. Transfer your fretting hand position intact from strings two and three over to strings one and two. Keep everything the same, including the fretting finger numbers you used in the original, just move the solo over one string. Try playing it on your own before you look at the version of "Lonesome Valley" transposed to the key of D below.

Lonesome Valley
moved over one string and transposed to the key of D

63

Once you're comfortable playing "Lonesome Valley" in both the original key of G and the transposed key of D, move the melody again, this time so your first note is on the open fourth string G. Just like last time, it's a simple case of moving your fretting hand position to a new set of strings. This version of "Lonesome Valley" is in the key of C.

Lonesome Valley

moved over one string the other way and transposed to the key of C

Let's recap what we've done so far. We learned "Lonesome Valley" in the original key of G and then moved our fretting hand position over one string and up in pitch to the key of D. Then we went back to our original key of G version and moved it over one string the other way and down in pitch to the key of C. Isn't that amazing? We're using the same hand position to play the same thing on different sets of strings and the result is the melody in a new key. Obviously you can transpose just about anything in the same way. Of course, if the melody spans all four strings, we have no where to go, but if the melody spans two strings, we can usually move it to two additional keys. If the melody spans three strings, we can usually move it to at least one other string location and an additional key. You can also change a few notes to make a melody fit onto two or three strings, which will thus make it more moveable.

It's important that you practice transposing to additional keys. At this point you should look back at all the songs you've already worked with and transpose them to other keys like we did with "Lonesome Valley."

The transposition chart below lists them all and what will be possible in the way of transposing using this string to string method. In the chart you'll find the previous songs listed alphabetically by title including the original key the song is in. To move a melody "up in pitch" means to start it on a higher pitched note/string than the original. For example, if the original first note is a 3rd string, 5th fret G, to move it up in pitch you'd start at the 2nd string, 5th fret D. By the same token, to move a melody "down in pitch" means to start it on a lower pitched note/string than the original. For example, if the original first note is a 3rd string, 5th fret G, to move it down in pitch you'd start at the 4th string, 5th fret C. Some listed songs (like "Crawdad Song" moved up in pitch) will transpose perfectly except for one or two notes. What should you do? Find a substitute note that works! Melodies that require more than one or two note substitutions are grayed out. That doesn't mean you shouldn't try to transpose to those positions. For example, "Down in the Willow Garden" can be easily moved up in pitch except for one note which recurrs again and again. See if you can figure it out or work around it. Go as far as you can with moving the written version and then try substituting notes. Try starting "Old Joe Clark" on the third string, open D note. What key will you be in? Good luck!

Transposition Chart Title	Page	Original Key	Move up in pitch to key of:	First Note	Move down in pitch to key of:	First Note
A Beautiful Life backup	56	G	X		C	2nd string, 3rd fret C
A Beautiful Life melody	56	G	D	2nd string, 5th fret D	C	4th string, 5th fret C
All the Good Times	27	B♭	F	1st string, 5th fret A	E♭	3rd string, 5th fret G
Aura Lee	29	G	D	2nd string, open A	C	4th string, open G
Banks of the Ohio	51	D	A	3rd string, 2nd fret E	X	
Bury Me Beneath #1	22	D	A	2nd string, 4th fret C♯	X	
Bury Me Beneath #2	48	C	G	3rd string, 5th fret G	X	
Crawdad Song	38	G	D	2nd string, 5th fret D	C	4th string, 5th fret C
Down in the Willow Garden	52	G	X		C	4th string, open G
East Virginia Blues	20	E	B	2nd string, 6th fret D♯	A	4th string, 6th fret C♯
In the Pines back-up	60	G	X		X	
In the Pines melody	60	G	D	1st string, 2nd fret F♯	C	3rd string, 2nd fret E
John Hardy	14	C	G	3rd string, 5th fret	X	
Liberty	35	D	X		G	2nd string, 2nd fret B
Long Journey Home	25	A♭	E♭	2nd string, 1st fret B♭	D♭	4th string, 1st fret A♭
New River Train back-up	58	D	A	2nd string, 4th fret C♯	G	4th string, 4th fret B
New River Train melody	58	D	A	2nd string, open A	G	4th string, open G
Nine Pound Hammer	36	G	D	2nd string, open A	C	4th string, open G
Old Joe Clark	32	A	X		D	2nd string, open A
Pass Me Not	53	G	X		X	
Ragtime Annie	34	D	X		G	4th string, 4th fret B
Somebody Touched Me	44	A	E	2nd string, 2nd fret B	D	4th string, 2nd fret A
When the Saints	42	G	D	2nd string, 5th fret D	C	4th string, 5th fret C
Will the Circle #1	16	A	X		D	4th string, 2nd fret A
Will the Circle #2	46	A	X		D	4th string, 2nd fret A

Work through all the previous songs before you go on. Eventually you should do the same with the songs that are coming up. As you learn new melodies and solos, try moving them to new keys. It'll give you a thorough understanding of how versatile the mandolin is and teach you much about its possibilities.

Transposing Up and Down the Fingerboard

"Lonesome Valley" has open-string (unfretted) notes, and as such we can only use the "string-to-string" method to transpose the melody to two additional keys. What if we need to play "Lonesome Valley" in a key other than G, D, or C? If all the notes of the melody are played fretted or in closed positions, our choices greatly increase. Then we can move the melody intact, up or down the fingerboard using "fret to fret" transposition.

Here's "Little Maggie." Learn the melody before you tackle the following solo. I didn't put fretting hand finger numbers into this version because I wanted you to continue working them out on your own. If you get stuck, you can check out the numbers on the solo and extrapolate from there. Your basic fretting hand position for the melody and the solo will be quite similar.

Little Maggie
basic version in the key of G

66

Learn the following "Little Maggie" solo in the key of G with the suggested fretting finger numbers. Pay particular attention to the fretting-hand positions the notes form. As you did with "Lonesome Valley," memorize the solo and the positions. You should be able to play it with your eyes closed.

Little Maggie
solo in the key of G

Let's say we need to be able to play this entire solo in the key of A. What we're going to do is move the whole solo, fretting hand fingers and positions, up (toward the bridge) two frets. Before you look at the solo transposed to the key of A below, try it on your own. If you get tangled up, go back to the key of G solo and work from there. Go through the process of teaching your head, eyes, and hands how to move up two frets and maintain the hand positions that you previously learned. This is what you'll have to do in the real world so you might as well practice it now. Once you get it, you'll be able to move the G solo, and ultimately any other melody or solo, up and down the fingerboard to as many as eight or more different positions and keys. Use the solo below to check yourself.

67

Little Maggie

solo transposed to the key of A

While you're at it, try moving "Little Maggie" up one more fret to the key of B♭. Then move the B♭ version down (toward the nut) two frets to the key of A♭. Work your way up and down the fingerboard to all the different keys you can reach. Try taking melodies you've already learned and change all the open-string notes to closed-string fretted notes. Once you can convert a melody to all fretted notes, it's easy to move it up and down the fingerboard to a variety of different keys.

Could we combine the techniques of fret to fret transposition with string to string transposition? I'm glad you asked! Go back to the key of G "Little Maggie" solo. Try moving it over one string, down in pitch, and play your first note on string three, fret one. Since the solo spans three strings, you should be able to move it over to at least one additional key. As always, try it in this new key of C on your own before you check yourself with the version below.

Little Maggie

solo moved over one string to the key of C

Now I'm getting excited! This exercise has shown you how to play "Little Maggie" in about sixteen different positions and keys. Well, not sixteen different keys because there are only twelve different keys. Still, it's an accomplishment of staggering proportions! As you progress, you'll find these same notes and positions from "Little Maggie" will help you find melodies and solos to an infinite number of melodies from the bluegrass, old time, and folk repertoires.

I'm guessing that you've had about enough of "Lonesome Valley" and "Little Maggie" for a while, so we'll move on to some other songs. Be sure that you understand the transposing process that we worked through, both string-to-string and fret-to-fret, with both "Lonesome Valley" and "Little Maggie." I know it can be conceptually and technically difficult, but you'll find that it's well worth the effort when in the future you'll be able to transpose just about any tune, lick, or solo to any key with ease. Yes, someday you will thank me!

Minor Chords

Minor chords are less common in bluegrass than major chords but they do occur and you need to know how to play them. You played an Em in "Aura Lee." "Shady Grove," a popular old-time song often performed by bluegrass bands, uses the Em and D chords shown below. Before we get to that, let's talk a little bit about chord theory.

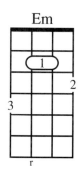 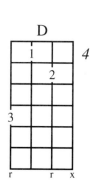 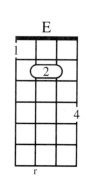

Previously we discussed moving one or two fingers and changing a chord from, say, E to E7. Chords like E, A, D, F, B♭, C, etc., are called "triads" because they are made up of three different tones, the first, third, and fifth tones of the chord's major scale. A "C" triad has C, E, and G notes in it, which are the first, third, and fifth tones of the chord's major scale. A "G" triad has the notes G, B, and D, or the first, third, and fifth tones of the G major scale. See below.

C major scale:	C	D	E	F	G	A	B	C
tone number	1	2	3	4	5	6	7	8

G major scale:	G	A	B	C	D	E	F♯	G
tone number	1	2	3	4	5	6	7	8

When we make a chord shape on the fingerboard, we're fretting some combination of these three notes. Since the mandolin has four strings, we often double up on one of the three tones of the triad. For example, the open C chord shown below has two E notes. (The numbers below the note names show which part of the scale each note is.)

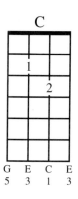 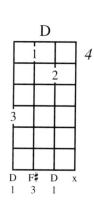

Many of the chords you have learned use only three of the mandolin's four strings, like the closed position D. You might expect a chord like this to only be made up of the first, third, and fifth tones of the D major scale: D, F♯, and A. In fact, this chord form leaves out one of the three tones of the triad. It includes two Ds, an F♯, but no A note. Why can we do this? We're mandolin players, that's why! As I mentioned before, it's become accepted in bluegrass music over the years to leave out chord tones and usually one or more of the other instruments in the band, the guitar, fiddle, bass, or banjo, supplies the missing tone. And, these types of chords are used as much for their rhythmic as their harmonic content.

The basic recipe for a major triad chord is that it is made up of the first, third, and fifth notes of the major scale that names it, even though a mandolin chord may not supply all three notes of the triad. But what about the minor chord?

Turns out a minor chord is also a triad, but with one note changed from the major triad. Minor chords contain the first, *flatted third*, and fifth notes of the associated major scale. To *flat* a note, we lower it one half step, or one fret on the fingerboard. So the notes of the C minor triad (written "Cm" and pronounced "C minor") are C, E♭, and G. The notes of the G minor chord are G, *B♭*, D. The notes of the E minor chord are E, *G♮*, B.

We can see this difference clearly if we compare the G major and G minor chord grids.

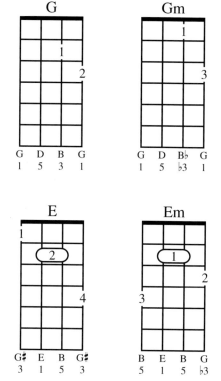

Most major chord forms can be made into minor chord forms by changing one finger and lowering the third of the chord by one half step or one fret. With some forms it's a little more complicated and we may have to move more than one finger. For example, look at the basic E chord below and notice that the third of the chord is played on both the first (fourth fret) and the fourth (first fret) strings. To make this E chord into an Em, we have to lower both of the thirds. That's easy enough and we may have to switch fingers, but when we lower the fourth string first fret G♯ by one fret, we get an open-string G natural. This is fine, but suddenly we have a chord with an open-string note so it's no longer a moveable chord. We solve the problem by switching notes around a bit. The changes preserve the moveable quality of the chord. See the Em below.

It's not important right now that you be able to lower thirds and substitute other notes as we did with this chord. It's more important that you understand that the difference between a major and minor chord is just one note, from natural third to flatted third. It's also important that you understand how this is reflected in the look of the chord. Compare other sets of major and minor chords that accompany "Wayfaring Stranger" and identify where the third tone is and how it gets flatted to make a minor chord. Eventually you'll be able to take any major chord form and make it into a minor, usually by moving only one finger down one fret.

What about seventh chords? There are different types of seventh chords, but chords like A7, D7, E♭7, etc. are often called *dominant seventh* chords. Like all chords, dominant seventh chords have a specific recipe. To make a dominant seventh chord we take a basic major triad and add the *flatted seventh note* of the chord's associated major scale. To get to the flatted seventh note, we take the *natural seven* and lower it one half step.

D major scale:	D	E	F♯	G	A	B	C♯	D
tone number	1	2	3	4	5	6	7	8

B♭ major scale:	B♭	C	D	E♭	F	G	A	B♭
tone number	1	2	3	4	5	6	7	8

The D7 chord includes the notes D, F♯, A and C♮. The C♮ ("C natural") note is one half step below the C♯ ("C sharp") note. The B♭7 chord includes the notes B♭, D, F, and A♭. Look at the chords to the right.

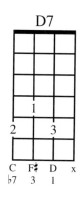

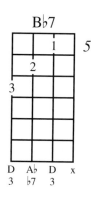

Again you'll see that some notes are missing in each case. This form of the D7 is missing the fifth note (A) of the D scale. The B♭7 form is missing both the first (B♭) and fifth notes (F). In both chords we still have the third, which is an important note because it tells us whether the chord is

71

major (natural third) or minor (flatted third). Both also have the seventh, which we need because it defines the "seventh" flavor of the chord.

As you progress, you'll come across other chords with different names, especially in other styles of music, like *minor seven, sixth, minor seven flat five, major seven, diminished, augmented,* and each will have a specific recipe, like those we've already discussed. For example, a minor seven chord includes a minor triad, 1, ♭3, 5 plus the flatted seventh note or ♭7. A minor seven chord would be named like this: Dm7 ("D minor seven") and include the notes D, F, A, C natural. Another you might see is a major seven. The recipe for a major seven is: 1, 3, 5, 7 and uses the natural seventh note of the associated major scale, not the flatted seventh as in C7. A C major seven chord would be written like this: CMaj7 or this: C△7 and include the notes C, E, G, B. The triangle (△) in the chord name means major seven. The recipe for a sixth chord is 1, 3, 5, 6. A C sixth chord would be written like this: C6 and include the notes C, E, G, A.

Practice the basic melody and chords to "Shady Grove" before you go on to the solo. The basic melody is played on strings two and three, and has open-string notes. Can you move it to other keys? Try a string-to-string move. The solo embellishes the melody with more notes. It's written here with open-string notes. Can you move the solo to other keys in the same way? We know that if we didn't have all those open-string notes, we'd be able to move it up, and possibly even down the neck, to a whole bunch of other keys. Try relocating the open-string notes to fretted notes on strings lower in pitch. Play them with your pinkie. If you're stumped, e-mail me at dix@musixnow.com and request that I e-mail you a copy of "Shady Grove solo, closed position."

David Grisman and Jerry Garcia recorded a wonderful version of this on their "Shady Grove" CD. I transcribed a book of lyrics, chords, and Jerry's guitar solos in standard notation and tablature ("Shady Grove" 97073) and Dan McGann put together a book of David's solos ("Shady Grove Mandolin Solos" 98101) . Both books are published by Mel Bay.

Shady Grove
basic version in the key of Em

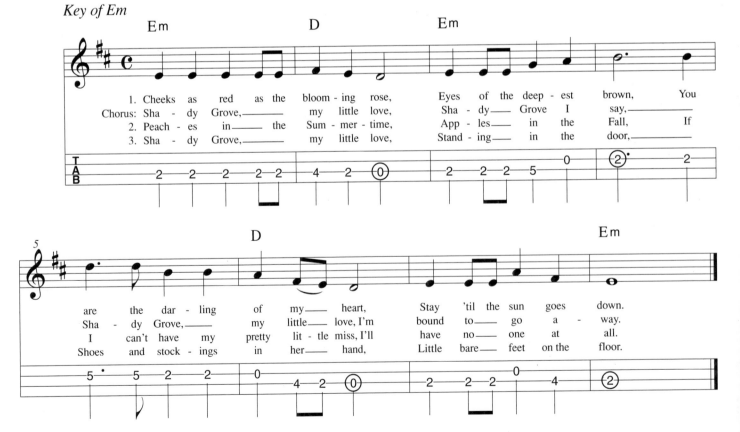

Shady Grove

solo in the key of Em

Wayfaring Stranger

"Wayfaring Stranger" uses Am and Dm chords, among others. Compare the major and minor chords below to see what notes change to move from one to the other. Learn the chords first, and then work on the solo. Use tremolo on the longer notes, mostly whole notes tied to a quarter note. All of the chords shown are "closed position" chords with no open strings, so the forms can be moved up and down the fingerboard to make different chords.

You may have noticed by now that we have learned more than one form for the same chord. Why bother? Because each form has a unique sound and place on the neck. We're building a repertoire of sounds and positions so we have more artistic choices. Feel free to substitute any other Dm, Am, etc., for the forms shown to the right. Just make sure that the names match. Any Dm will work for any other Dm, but a Dm7 is a completely different chord. Same with A7 and AMaj7. One cannot be substituted for the other.

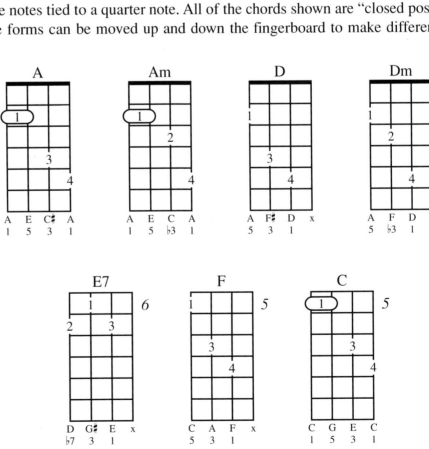

Wayfaring Stranger

basic version in the key of Am

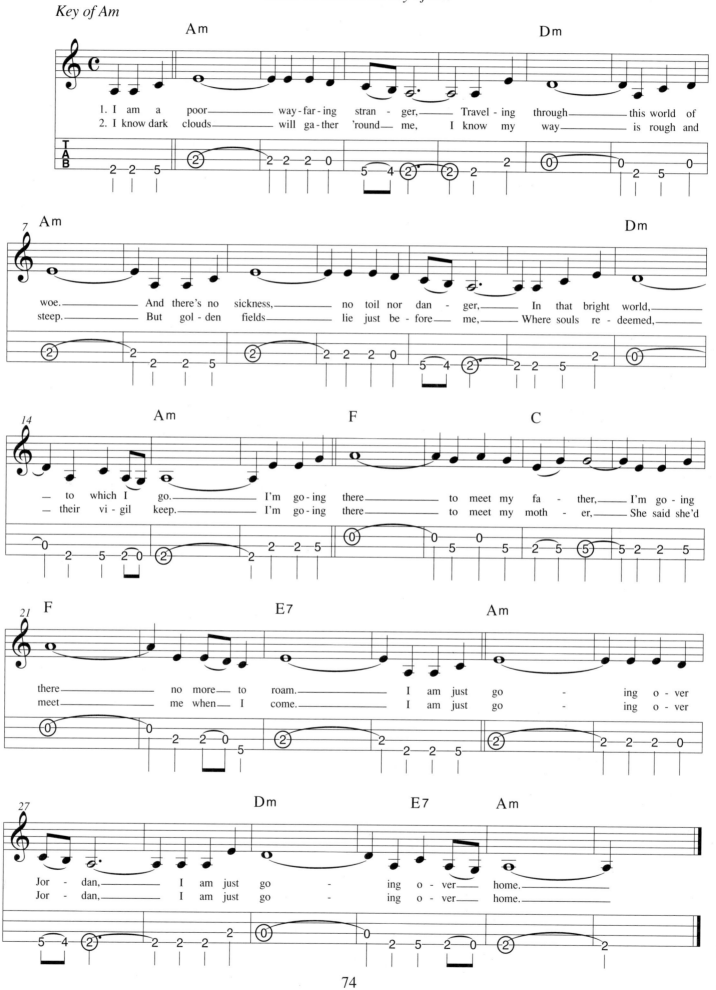

The "Wayfaring Stranger" solo is written in closed position with first and second endings. I changed one note in m9 & m25 to make it a little easier to move up or down the fingerboard and transpose to other keys, which you should be sure to try. I suggest tremolo on notes longer than quarters for both the basic melody and the solo.

Wayfaring Stranger
solo in the key of Am

Up to now we've played eighth notes with alternating down and up pick strokes. However, Bill Monroe, and just about every other past and current bluegrass mandolin player, often used all down-strokes when playing at slow and moderate tempos to make the notes punch out more, to sound louder and more intense. Try the solo to "Wayfaring Stranger" below first with all down-strokes and then with alternating downs and ups. (Use tremolo on the longer notes.) Notice the differences in sound between the two ways of picking. Which do you like better? Review all the other solos in the book and try them with all down-strokes.

Bluesy Solos & The Moveable Blues

Bill Monroe often talked about the huge influence blues music had in his version of bluegrass. Certainly many of the themes and forms of American blues are evident in the bluegrass repertoire. But Bill was also describing his bluesy approach to singing and playing where he included "blue" notes. What are blue notes? We can find the blue notes in any major scale by flatting the third and seventh tones. The blue notes in the C major scale are E♭ and B♭.

C major scale:	C	D	E	F	G	A	B	C
tone number	1	2	3	4	5	6	7	8

Here's the same scale with blue notes:

	C	D	E♭	F	G	A	B♭	C
	1	2	♭3	4	5	6	♭7	8

The blue notes in the G major scale are B♭ and F natural.

G major scale:	G	A	B	C	D	E	F♯	G
tone number	1	2	3	4	5	6	7	8

Here's the same scale with blue notes:

	G	A	B♭	C	D	E	F	G
	1	2	♭3	4	5	6	♭7	8

Photo by Dix Bruce

Bowlback "taterbug" mandolins

If we're playing in the key of C, we can add E♭ and B♭ notes here and there to add to the bluesy flavor of a melody or solo. If we're playing in the key of G, we can add B♭ and F natural notes to add bluesy flavor. The original, unflatted, third and seventh notes might also still be used. "Moveable Blues," inspired by Bill Monroe, uses lots of flatted thirds (B♭) and sevenths (F natural) from the G major scale. We'll learn it first in the key of G, as shown below, to hear how these flatted thirds and sevenths sound.

Moveable Blues

Key of G

by Dix Bruce

"Moveable Blues" is written is a closed position so we can move it later on. So, all the notes are fretted and suggested fingerings and pick directions are indicated. Stick to these suggestions and it'll be easier to move the whole melody later. Your pinkie will get some exercise as it frets notes high on the first and fourth strings in m1, m2, m9, and m10.

"Moveable Blues" also includes our first *triplets,* in m3 & m11. With triplets we fit three eighth notes in the space of one beat. Think first of a quarter note. We'd count quarter notes in a 4/4 measure like this: "one, two, three, four," and each quarter note occupies the space of one beat. If we filled that same measure with eighth notes, we'd fit two eighth notes in the space of each quarter note and we'd count them like this: "one and, two and, three and, four and." With triplets, we fit *three* notes in the space of one beat and count them like this: "one-trip-let, two-trip-let, three-trip-let, four-trip-let." We pick a note on each syllable: "one-trip-let." Listen to "Triplet Demo" on the CD. I suggest that you play triplets with a "down-up-down, down-up-down, down-up-down, down-up-down" picking pattern.

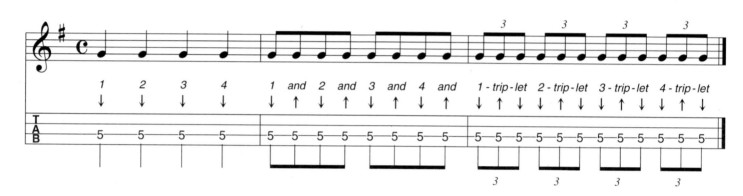

Once you have memorized "Moveable Blues" and its fretting hand position in the key of G, try moving it up the fingerboard to different positions and keys. The key of B♭, three frets up the fingerboard, is a good place to start. I'm sure you'll hit some clinkers now and then, but give it a chance. If you get stuck, go back to the G version and review. If you can play it in B♭, you can play it anywhere you can reach! The obvious next step is the key of B, one more fret up the neck. As a bluegrass mandolinist, you'll be expected to be able to play in B, so now's a good time to explore the B position with this and other melodies. Be sure to try A, C, A♭, D, etc. (If you can't figure it out in B♭, drop me an e-mail, dix@musixnow.com, and I'll send you a copy of the music and TAB.) Once you can move the melody up and down the neck comfortably, try moving the original G version down one string so that your first note is the fourth string fifth fret C. This position will put you in the key of C, and you can play the entire melody (except for two notes). You'll run out of fingerboard real estate on the last note in m2 and m10. What, oh what shall you do? Improvise! Suggestion: play the next to last note in each measure twice or substitute another note you like. When you have the C melody nailed, moved it up the neck to every key you can reach, C♯/D♭, D, D♯/E♭, E, F, etc., and so on.

If you really want "Moveable Blues" to have that Bill Monroe-esque feel, try playing all the notes, except maybe the triplets, with down-strokes. That's how Bill got that almost rock and roll intensity from a little acoustic mandolin.

Man of Constant Sorrow

Since its inclusion on the soundtrack to the film "Oh Brother Where Art Thou?," the song "Man of Constant Sorrow" has enjoyed a wave of new popularity far beyond bluegrass and folk fans. Not only is it a wonderful song, it's familiar again to a wide range of audiences. Here's the vocal version, followed by a mandolin solo. Learn the basic version before you tackle the solo. Ralph and Carter Stanley's version of this folk song is the classic but the song has been recorded hundreds of times by many other bluegrass, country, and folk artists. The film version by the Soggy Bottom Boys may prove to be the new classic.

The solo has open-string notes and is not moveable up and down the fingerboard. However, if you change all the open-string notes to fretted notes, you can move it anywhere. Make that an exercise on the solo after you've mastered it as written. I had Bill Monroe's sound in mind when I wrote this solo. Like the "Moveable Blues," this solo should be played with intensity. Try it with the usual up and down pick directions and then with all down strokes. Obviously in the second part you'll encounter tremolo and there you'll have to use upstrokes as well.

The two halves of the solo are structured differently to demonstrate two different approaches. The first is all single string, the second has double stop tremolo passages. You can play one half or the other twice through to make a complete solo. That'll give you two different solos to the song.

Remember that the numbers between the standard and tablature staves are suggested fretting finger numbers. The two stacked numbers in the second part, m11—m15, show fretting fingers for double stops. The top number is the finger used to fret the higher note, the lower number for the lower. The G7 chord in m14 reflects the F♮ note in the double stop. If you add an F♮ note to a G chord, you change the chord to a G7.

As I mentioned, this solo has open-string notes and because of that it cannot be moved up and down the fingerboard and transposed to other keys until you substitute fretted notes for the open-string notes. You can, however, move the solo as written with open strings, or the melody for that matter, from string to string and transpose it to at least one other key. As you did with previous solos, start "Man of Constant Sorrow" on the third string, fifth fret. What key have you transposed the solo to? Now try starting the solo on the first string fifth fret. You'll run into some problems, but they are solvable problems. For example, in m8, notes two and three (the G eighth notes in the original solo) are not playable because you've run out of strings. What should you do? Improvise! Find notes that work. How about simply playing the first string, fifth fret A here? Works for me.

In part two of the solo you'll also run out of strings in m11, m15-m19. Here you can play only the lower note of the double stop, and again, improvise where you have to. What key is this transcribed solo in?

It's important that you take all the solos and melodies in this book and try to move them around in the ways demonstrated. Always try to use what you know to lead you to things you don't know. This type of transposition in invaluable to any mandolinist, and the process of experimenting with it will quickly teach you more about how the mandolin works than two hundred pages of my deathless prose. So, do yourself a favor and try to move everything you learn from string to string and up and down the fingerboard to as many different keys as you can. Be sure to identify the key you are transposing to.

It's also important to stretch your abilities and improvise when you run up against a musical problem, like we discovered in transposing the solo to "Man of Constant Sorrow." When you hit a brick wall, go around it and get on down the road. You can go over it, around to the left, around to the right, or take a diagonal. It's up to you and your creativity.

Extra-credit assignment: Both "Moveable Blues" and "Man of Constant Sorrow" are written in the key of G. Try fitting parts of the melody of "Moveable Blues," with all its blue notes, over the chord changes to "Man of Constant Sorrow." Match passages to common chord changes, e.g., plug a G chord passage into a G chord space.

You may have noticed that we haven't transposed any fiddle tunes to different keys. That's because, by and large, fiddle tunes are performed in a set key. Unlike vocals where we have to accommodate different vocal ranges, fiddle tunes were mostly written to be played on fiddle in keys that work best on the fiddle: D, A, G, etc.

Guitarists often use capos on fiddle tunes to play in keys they like while still providing the fiddler with chords in his or her fiddle key. As a mandolinist, you'll generally play fiddle tunes in the fiddler's key, and nowhere else.

One of the most important things you can do to further your continuing education in bluegrass mandolin is to listen to recordings of the great players and bands on CD. Find players and sounds that really excite you, whether that's Monroe, Flatt & Scruggs (you'll have to make do with CDs), David Grisman, Del McCoury, or Nickel Creek. If you love the music, the song, or solo, you'll listen to it over and over, until you get those sounds into your brain, heart and soul. To really understand bluegrass and be able to play it, you almost need to "memorize" your favorite players and their music. So, crank up the Victrola and also get out and experience music that you love in a live setting.

Photo by Dix Bruce

The master's hand with his master model Lloyd Loar F-5

Man of Constant Sorrow

basic version in the key of G

3. It's fare thee well, my own true lover,
I never expect to see again.

For I'm bound to ride, that northern railroad,
Perhaps I'll die upon this train.

4. You can bury me, In some deep valley,
For many years where I may lay.
Then you may learn, To love another,
While I am sleeping in my grave.

5. Maybe your friends think, I'm just a stranger,
My face you never will see no more.
But there is one promise that is given,
I'll meet you on God's golden shore.

Man of Constant Sorrow

solo in the key of G

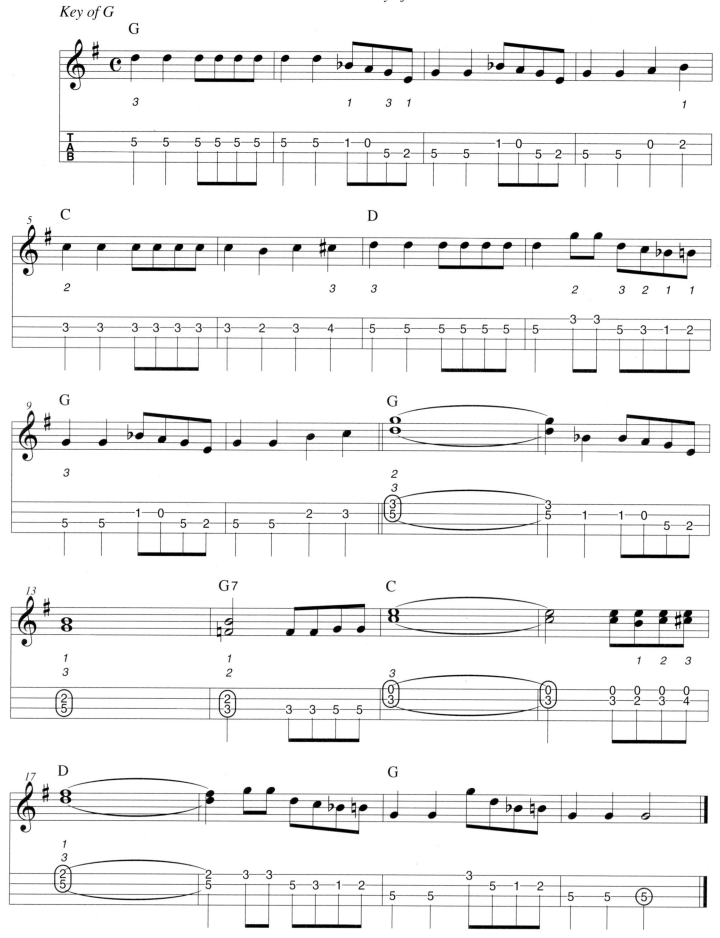

Kickoffs and Turnarounds

A *kickoff* is the same as an introduction. In bluegrass, a kickoff is often the last line or last several measures of the tune. This may also be referred to as a *turnaround*. In addition, a turnaround is often any melody played over a I-V-I ("one-five-one") chord progression. In the key of G that would be G-D-G. The kickoff doesn't have to be a turnaround, especially if the song doesn't have those chord changes in its last few bars.

Here's a kickoff to "Man of Constant Sorrow" which uses the melody and chords from m6-m10 of the solo you just learned.

"Man of Constant Sorrow" kickoff

Kickoffs don't have to quote the melody of the song they are introducing, but you'll never go wrong with the melody. When you listen to classic bluegrass bands you'll find that the mandolinist often takes melodic liberties. Here are three kickoffs to "Will the Circle Be Unbroken" in A. Try them first on "Circle" and then on other songs in A. Transpose them to other keys as well. Your only limitations will be if the other songs are in a different meter, like 3/4. But we'll learn a few of those too.

The first two kickoffs to "Will the Circle Be Unbroken" in A use single strings, and the third uses double stops. You'll notice that they all end with a whole note. Mandolinists usually extend the kickoff here and blend back into rhythm playing. It would be rare to end a kickoff or solo abruptly like this; you'd want to gradually transition back into your rhythm role. Just be sure to taper off so the vocalist knows when to come in. For more information on this subject, refer to "Transitions Back into Rhythm" on page 49. The kickoff examples on the CD demonstrate what I mean.

"Will the Circle Be Unbroken" kickoff #1

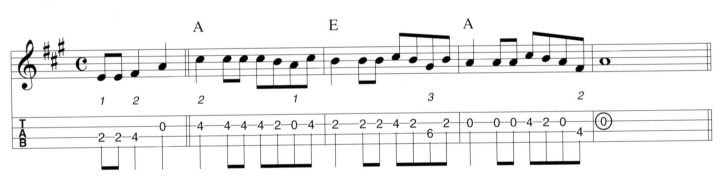

"Will the Circle Be Unbroken" kickoff #2

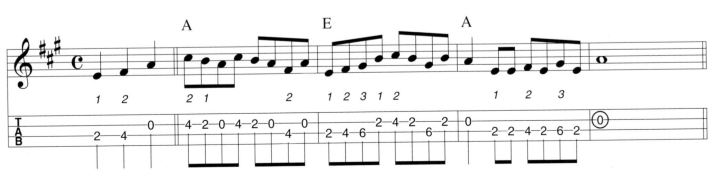

"Will the Circle Be Unbroken" kickoff #3

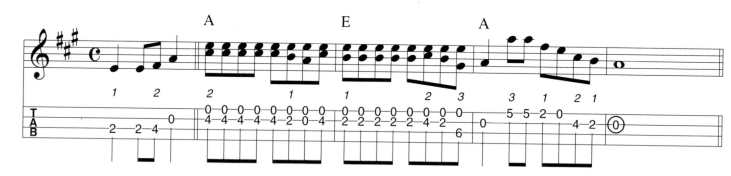

As you can see by now, kickoffs are like a partial solo. As such, similar forms are often used between verses when a full solo isn't needed. We wouldn't call it a "kickoff" anymore because we're not kicking off a tune. Rather, it might be called a turnaround or a partial solo. Try using these kickoffs as turnarounds between verses in songs.

Here are three kickoffs to "Bury Me Beneath the Willow" in the key of D. The first two are similar to ones you've previously learned. The last one is in a closed position and moveable up and down the fingerboard. Can you move this kickoff from string to string?

"Bury Me Beneath the Willow" kickoff 1

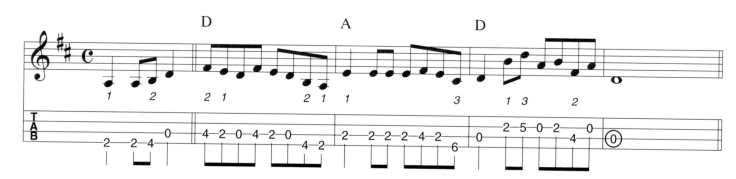

"Bury Me Beneath the Willow" kickoff 2

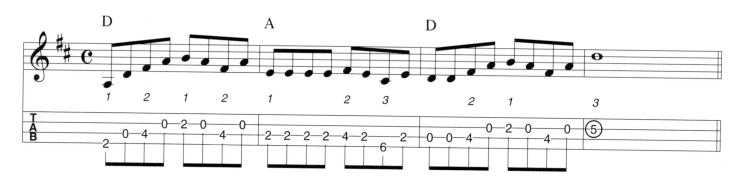

"Bury Me Beneath the Willow" kickoff 3

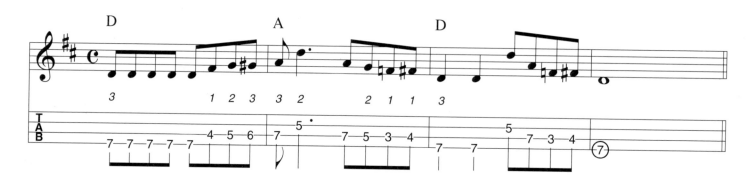

84

You've previously worked out "Lonesome Valley" in three keys: G, D and C. Here are two kickoffs in C. The first uses some open strings. Can you turn it into a closed position kickoff? Hint: you'll have to change at least one note.

The second kickoff is in closed position and a version of kickoff one played an octave higher with double stops. Move both kickoffs from C to the keys of G and D. Don't forget tremolo on the longer notes.

"Lonesome Valley" kickoff 1

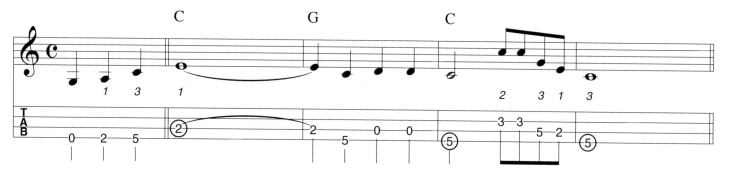

"Lonesome Valley" kickoff 2

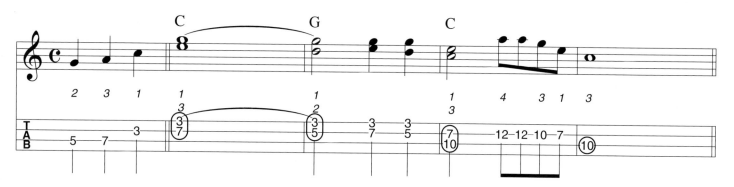

We don't want to forget songs in waltz time or 3/4. Here's a couple of kickoffs for "In the Pines" in G. The first is an *arpeggiated* passage with all chord tones. An *arpeggio* is simply a sequence of chord tones. The second kickoff is in a closed position and uses double stop tremolo.

"In the Pines" kickoff 1

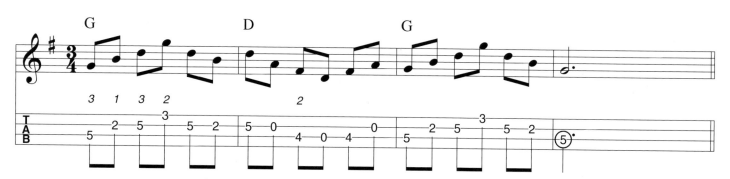

"In the Pines" kickoff 2

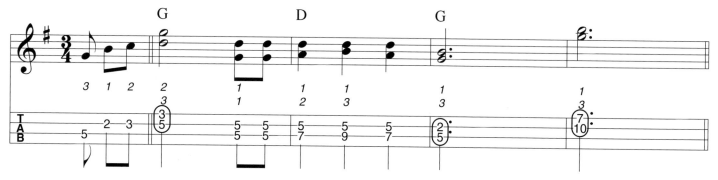

We'll wrap things up with two more 3/4 or waltz time kickoffs, this time on "All the Good Times" in the key of B♭. Both are in closed positions. The first works out of the B♭ chop chord and the fingering is a little tricky. Again it uses arpeggiated chord tones. The second is in a lower position and has some tremoloed notes.

"All the Good Times" kickoff 1.

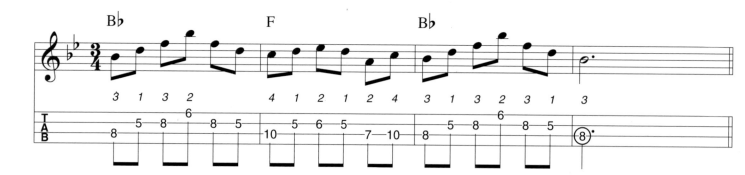

"All the Good Times" kickoff 2.

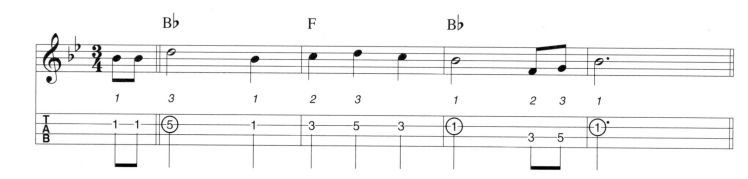

Jamming

One of the most exciting aspects of bluegrass music is that jamming is an integral part of the scene. Bluegrassers love to get together and play music, swap tunes and licks, and generally have a great time sharing their love of bluegrass. So, as soon as possible, **get thee to a jam session!** You will learn a thousand times faster than just playing on your own. Bluegrass players always jam at festivals and often in the parking lot at concerts. It's a way to meet people you can play with and learn from. It's also a great way to exercise everything you've been working on in this book, and then some! Most communities have public jams at restaurants, schools, or bars where you can lurk and listen until you're ready to jump in.

If you don't feel that you're accomplished enough yet to play along in a jam session, just listen off to the side and watch how people jam. Take note of the repertoire and start learning it. Chances are the songs and tunes will include the greatest hits of the classic bluegrass artists like Monroe, Ralph and Carter Stanley, Flatt & Scruggs, Jimmy Martin, The Country Gentlemen, Tony Rice, J.D. Crowe, etc. These tunes make up a kind of standard bluegrass performing and jamming repertoire. Tom Diamant, a musician, DJ at KPFA-FM (Berkeley, CA) and old friend of mine, recently reminded me of how powerful the bluegrass repertoire is. He said, "You can go to a bluegrass jam in any part of the world and they'll play the same Monroe and Stanley songs and fiddle tunes that you know. No matter what the local language is, you'll be able communicate with bluegrass players anywhere in the world with bluegrass standards." He spoke a parable.

Jams *do* vary somewhat depending upon the participants, and you'll find them to be fluid over time. Some might be more old timey, others more modern. Some jams may favor instrumentals and fiddle tunes, others might include western swing material. Some may frown on any of the above. Generally though, they'll share a common repertoire. Just scope it out. Bluegrass festivals offer you the wonderful advantage of a smorgasbord of jams all going on at the same time. Walk around and take your pick!

Use common courtesy and common sense. Sometimes it might not be appropriate for you to join in. In such a case, listen and learn. Usually though, people will be outwardly welcoming and eventually invite you to choose a song. There are general rules of jam etiquette. They come down to this: try to be a good guest and a good band member. Start out at the edge of the jam until you feel comfortable or brave. It's always OK to quietly play along. You don't have to lead a tune, but that can be where the real fun begins.

Once you're in the swim and it's your turn to choose a song or tune, be prepared. Nobody wants to wait ten minutes while you decide what to play or sing. Have at least a couple of tunes ready in case your first choice isn't known by the group. Keep your fellow jammers in mind when you choose a tune. Try to make it something simple and familiar. It doesn't have to be one of the "bluegrass greatest hits" as long as the chords are relatively easy or similar to something well-known. If you're at a mixed jam with a range of players' abilities, unknown songs with lots of chord changes will chase people away. You'll become a "jam buster." However, it may be appropriate to try more challenging material if the players are so inclined. Try to gauge what the group is interested in playing. Also, know the key that you perform a song or tune in. Again, be prepared. Write out a list of jam songs and keys and take it with you to the jam. Remember that bluegrassers tend to like C and the sharp keys, especially G, A, and D though there's no reason to avoid keys like F, B♭ etc., if that's your singing key.

Above all, be a supportive jam member. Listen when your fellow jammers play and sing. Don't be so preoccupied with your next solo or song that you don't give them the attention they deserve. Help them to play or sing their best. Support them in the way you'd like to be supported. You'll no doubt run into players who practice their solo during your vocal or who play too loud and just play all the time and aren't into sharing the sand box. Maybe they'll learn someday. Most people would rather play with you, a supportive player who listens!

So Long!

That brings us to the end of *Getting into Bluegrass Mandolin*. You've worked on a whole lot of things that will help you become a bluegrass mandolin player and you've come along way. From chords with open strings to the Big Bad Bluegrass Chop Chord, from simple single string melodies to challenging closed position bluegrass solos that you can play in any key. Along the way you worked on tablature, tremolo, double stops, fiddle tunes, transposing, composing bluegrass solos, and playing the blues. What a great start! Of course there's so much more to explore, and much of it I'll put into my *Bluegrass Mandolin Solos* book, which I'll finish as soon as I get this off to the printer. It'll have a whole bunch of great solos, more tremolo and double stop work, more transposing and solos is all keys, cross picking, fiddle tunes, waltzes, blues and more. Be sure to watch for it.

In the meantime, visit me online at www.musixnow.com. There's lots of music, tab, and MP3s to download. You can also check out my other books, CDs, and videos online. They cover a range of ability, interest and styles. For more work with fiddle tunes, try *BackUP TRAX: Old Time & Fiddle Tunes Vol.1* (94339BCD). It includes music, chords and tab to some of the most popular fiddle tunes in the style. You'll learn them by playing along with a band on the CD at both slow and regular speed. The band will back *you* up all night long and help you to hone your fiddle tune craft. We also have a *BackUP TRAX: Swing & Jazz Edition* (94344BCD). Don't forget my *Famous Mandolin Pickin' Tunes* (98420BCD) for a great repertoire of all kinds of mandolin tunes, from classical to jazz and bluegrass.

That's all for now. Keep on picking!

Dix Bruce

By the way, I used the Finale software package to write all the music and tab in this book. It's a serious tool for the serious musician. I recommend it!

Chord Dictionary

Reminder: All closed-position chords are moveable up and down the neck. Not all possible forms are shown for each chord, as they may be difficult to make high on the fingerboard. Be sure to try moving all forms up and down the fingerboard as far as possible on your mandolin. The "r" under a chord grid shows where the chord's "root" is located. This root note names the chord, and as you move a closed chord form, this note will identify and name the new chord. Some chord forms will not include a root note. Chords with two names separated by a slash (C♯/D♭, A♯7/B♭7, F♯m/G♭m) are "enharmonic" names for the same chord.

Major Chords

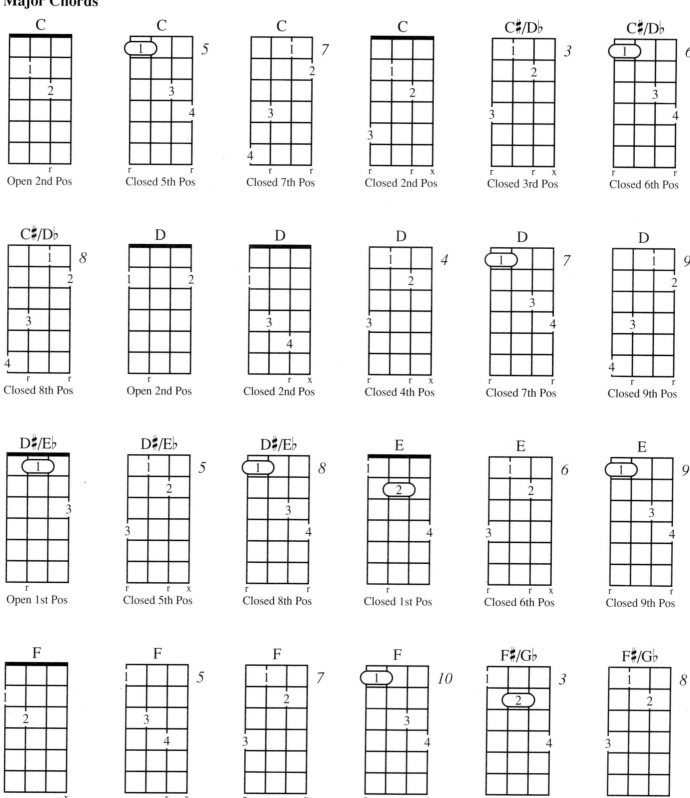

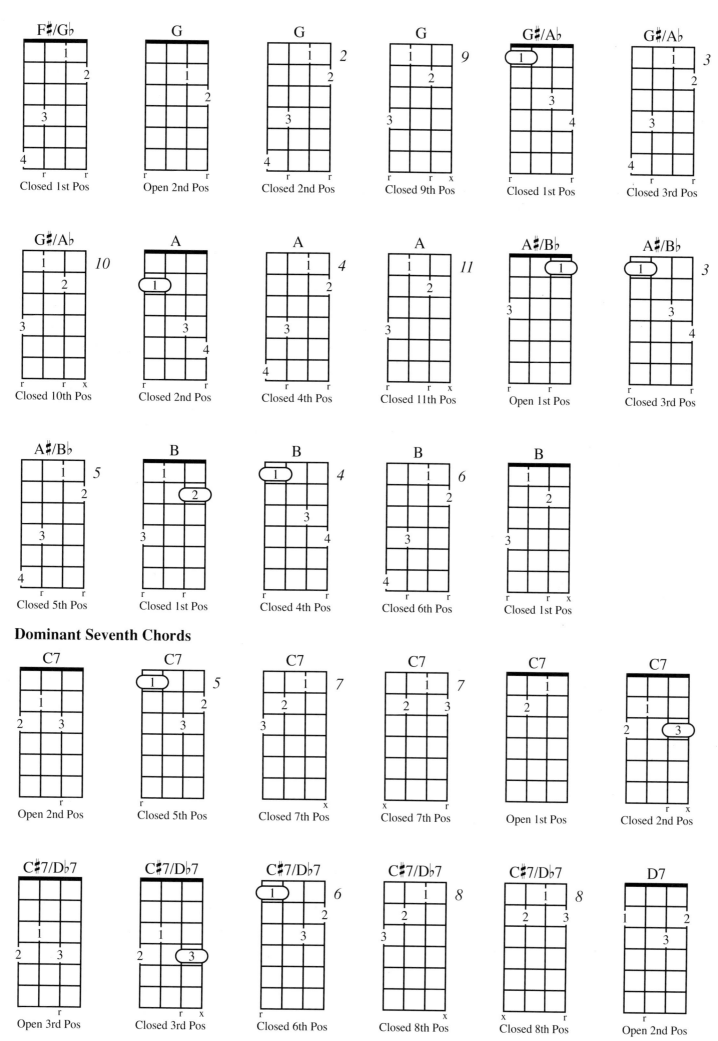

Dominant Seventh Chords

89

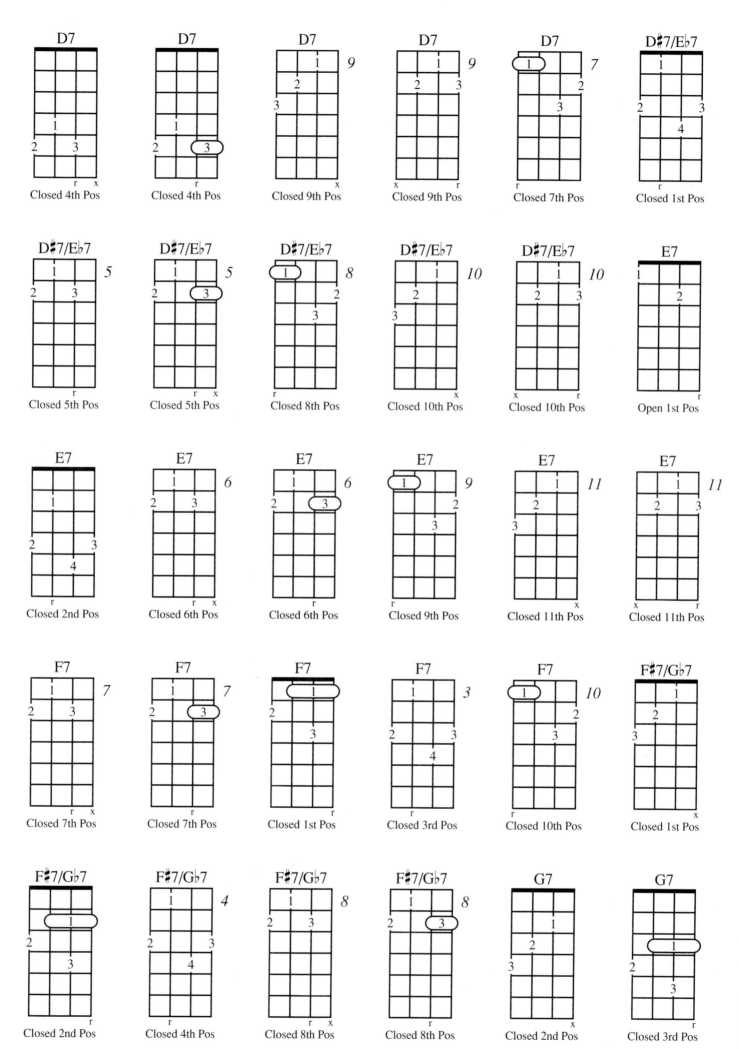

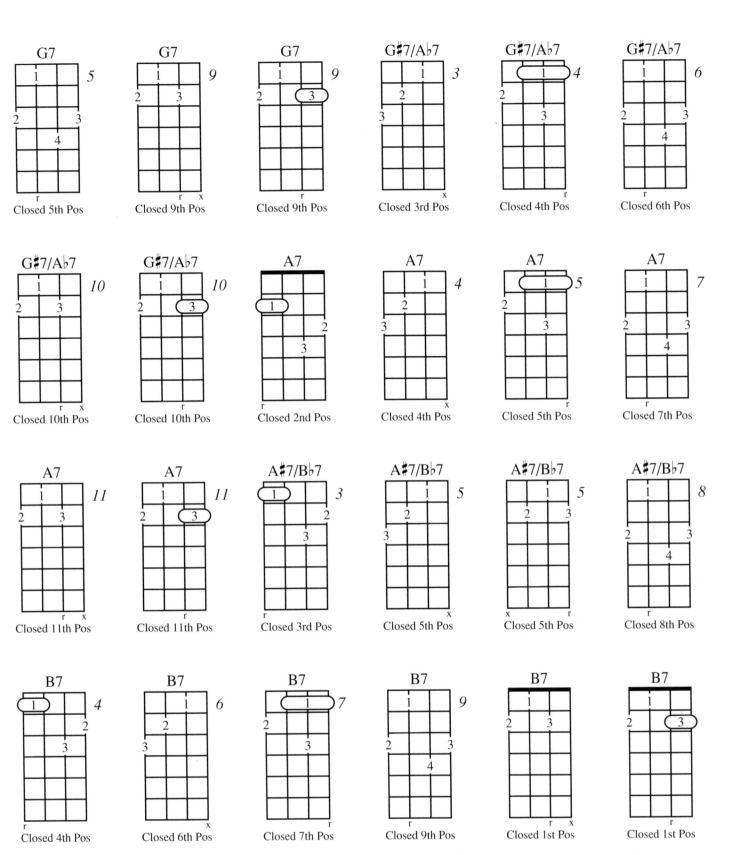

Minor Chords

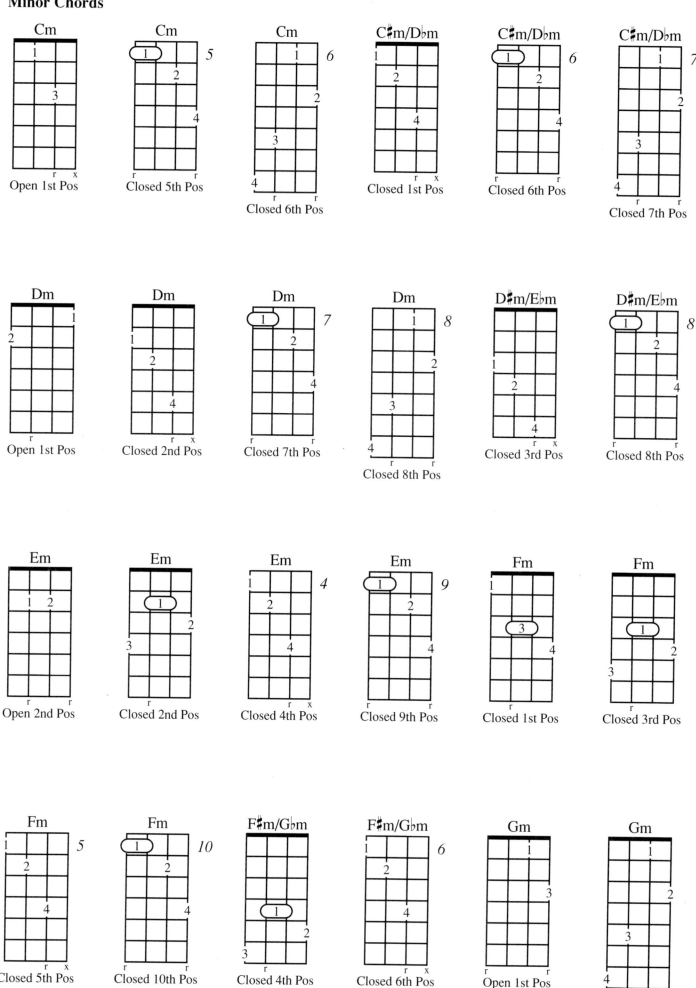

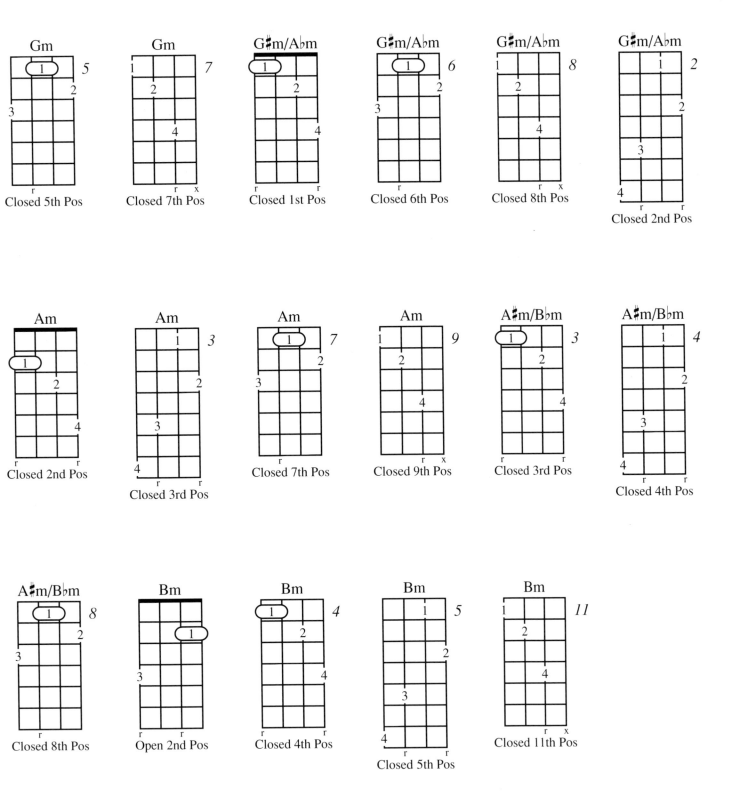

Gm — Closed 5th Pos

Gm — Closed 7th Pos

G#m/Abm — Closed 1st Pos

G#m/Abm — Closed 6th Pos

G#m/Abm — Closed 8th Pos

G#m/Abm — Closed 2nd Pos

Am — Closed 2nd Pos

Am — Closed 3rd Pos

Am — Closed 7th Pos

Am — Closed 9th Pos

A#m/Bbm — Closed 3rd Pos

A#m/Bbm — Closed 4th Pos

A#m/Bbm — Closed 8th Pos

Bm — Open 2nd Pos

Bm — Closed 4th Pos

Bm — Closed 5th Pos

Bm — Closed 11th Pos

Index

About the Author

Dix Bruce is a musician and writer from the San Francisco Bay area. He has authored over forty books, recordings, and videos for Mel Bay Publications. He edited *Mandolin World News,* David Grisman's legendary mandolin magazine, from 1978 to 1984. Dix performs and does studio work on guitar, mandolin, and banjo and has recorded two LPs with mandolin legend Frank Wakefield, eight big band CDs with the Royal Society Jazz Orchestra, his own collection of American folk songs entitled *My Folk Heart* on which he plays guitar, mandolin, autoharp and sings, and a CD of string swing and jazz entitled *Tuxedo Blues.* He contributed two original compositions to the soundtrack of Harrod Blank's acclaimed documentary film *Wild Wheels.* He has released four CDs of traditional American songs and originals with guitarist Jim Nunally, most recently a collection of "brother duet" style recordings entitled *Brothers at Heart.* Dix arranged, composed, and played mandolin on the soundtracks to four different editions of the best selling computer game *The Sims.*

Photo by Gene Tortora